REBECCA STEFOFF

With thanks to Priscilla Spears, Ph.D., for her expert review of the manuscript.

Marshall Cavendish Benchmark
99 White Plains Road
Tarrytown, New York 10591-9001
www.marshallcavendish.us
Text copyright © 2008 by Rebecca Stefoff
Illustrations copyright © 2008 by Marshall Cavendish Corporation
Illustrations by Robert Romagnoli
All rights reserved. No part of this book may be reproduced or utilized in any form or by any means electronic or mechanical including photocopying, recording, or by any information storage and retrieval system, without permission from the copyright holders.

All Web sites were available and accurate when this book was sent to press.

Editor: Karen Ang
Publisher: Michelle Bisson
Art Director: Anahid Hamparian
Series Designer: Patrice Sheridan

Library of Congress Cataloging-in-Publication Data

Stefoff, Rebecca, date
The Fungus kingdom / by Rebecca Stefoff.
p. cm. — (Family trees)
Summary: "Explores the habitats, life cycles, and other characteristics of organisms in the Fungus Kingdom"—Provided by publisher.
Includes bibliographical references and index.
ISBN 978-0-7614-2696-7
1. Fungi—Juvenile literature. I. Title. II. Series.

QK603.5.S74 2008
579.5--dc22

2007003485

Front cover: Blood-red Marasmius in the Costa Rican rainforest
Title page and back cover: An amanita mushroom
Photo research by Candlepants, Incorporated
Front cover: Michael and Patricia Fogden / Minden Pictures
The photographs in this book are used by permission and through the courtesy of: *Minden Pictures:* Michael Hutchinson/npl, 29; Colin Monteath/Hedgehog House, 31 (top); Eddy Marissen/Foto Natura, 31 (bottom); Jan Vermeer, 43; Michael & Patricia Fogden, 44, 53, 54; Konrad Wothe, 45; Mark Moffett, 63; Piotr Naskrecki, 66. *SuperStock:* Ingram Publishing, 3, 36, back cover; age fotostock, 56; Stock Image, 81. *Corbis:* Owen Franken, 74; John Farmar/Cordaiy Photo Library Ltd., 83. *Peter Arnold:* Darlyne A. Murawski, 6. *Photo Researchers, Inc.:* SPL, 9, 18; Edward Kinsman, 10; G. Tomsich, 11; Sinclair Stammers/ SPL, 20; AJPhoto, 27; Dr. P. Marazzi, 32; Jean-Marie Bassot, 38; LSHTM, 48; Dr. Jeremy Burgess, 51, 58; Jeff Lepore, 59, 75; Eye of Science, 61; Nigel Cattlin, 65; Gregory K. Scott, 69; Volker Steger, 79. *Visuals Unlimited:* John Taylor, 26; Dick Poe, 30; James Richardson, 33; Dr. Dennis Kunkel, 39, 41; Dr. Fred Hossler, 70. *The Image Works:* David R. Frazier, 72. *Envision:* Rita Maas, 73. *AP Images:* 77. *Hans Steur:* 35, 21. *Reprinted with permission from Mycologia.:* © The Mycological Society of America, 22.

Printed in Malaysia
135642

CHILDREN'S ROOM

CONTENTS

INTRODUCTION	Classifying Life	7
	The Five Kingdoms Family Tree	16
CHAPTER ONE	A Kingdom of Their Own	19
CHAPTER TWO	What Is a Fungus?	37
CHAPTER THREE	Scavengers, Partners, and Parasites	57
CHAPTER FOUR	Living with Fungi	71
Glossary		84
Fungus Family Tree		86
Find Out More		88
Bibliography		91
Index		92

3 9222 02 964930 3

The mushrooms at the base of this tree are just a tiny part of the huge fungus that spreads for miles beneath the forest floor.

INTRODUCTION

Classifying Life

The biggest living thing in the world is almost invisible, unless you know where to look. That's because it lives underground. It measures 24.6 miles (39.6 kilometers) from side to side and covers 3.7 square miles (9.6 square kilometers)—an area larger than 1,600 football fields. It has billions of tentacles that suck the life out of trees. It's at least 2,400 years old. And if it isn't a single huge organism, then it's a nest of tightly packed clones.

Is this something from a science-fiction movie? No, just a giant fungus called the honey mushroom. Scientists call it an *Armillaria ostoyae.* In 2000 it was discovered in the Blue Mountains of eastern Oregon. Before that time, the title of world's largest organism had been held by honey mushrooms in Michigan and, later, the state of Washington. An *Armillaria* even larger than the Blue Mountain monster could be found any day by mycologists, the scientists who study mushrooms and other fungi.

The *Armillaria ostoyae* lives just beneath the surface of the forest floor and stretches down to a depth of about 1 yard (about 1 meter). It spreads by growing along tree roots and by sending out rhizomorphs, long, narrow

root-like filaments, or threads. "If you could take away the soil and look at it, it's just one big heap of fungus with all these filaments that go out under the surface," says Catherine Parks, a research scientist who found the giant fungus when she was investigating the deaths of trees from root disease. "The fact that an organism like this has been growing in the forest for thousands of years really expands our view of the forest ecosystem and how it functions."

Fungi are vital to most ecosystems, even if they are often overlooked—or invisible. Mushrooms and toadstools are familiar fungi, but they make up just part of the fungus kingdom. Molds, mildews, smuts, rusts, blights, and yeasts are fungi, too. The unpleasant-sounding names were coined to describe plant diseases, and it's true that fungi attack plants. But fungi also form partnerships with plants that allow plants to thrive, and they are a source of foods and medicines. Most important, fungi are a key part of the world's clean-up crew, working to prevent the planet from being covered with dead plants and animals.

From an underground *Armillaria* that covers acres, to the delicious portobello and shiitake mushrooms in the supermarket, to tiny single-celled yeasts used in making bread and beer, fungi come in a vast variety of forms. To understand the place of the fungus kingdom in the natural world, it helps to know something about how scientists classify living things.

THE INVENTION OF TAXONOMY

Science gives us tools for making sense of the natural world. One of the most powerful tools is classification, which means organizing things in a pattern according to their differences and similarities. Since ancient times, scientists who study living things have been developing taxonomy, a classification system for organisms. Taxonomists group together living things that share certain features, setting them apart from other organisms with different features.

A nineteenth-century drawing of fungi shows details seen only through a microscope.

Taxonomy is hierarchical, which means that it is arranged in levels of categories. The highest levels include many kinds of organisms. These large categories are divided into smaller categories, which in turn are divided into still smaller ones. The smallest category of all is the species, a single kind of organism.

The idea behind taxonomy is simple, but the world of living things is complex and full of surprises. Taxonomy is not a fixed pattern. It keeps changing to reflect new knowledge or ideas. Over time, scientists have developed rules for adjusting the pattern even when they disagree on the details.

One of the first taxonomists was the ancient Greek philosopher Aristotle (384–322 BCE), who investigated many branches of science, including biology. Aristotle arranged living things on a sort of ladder, or scale. At the bottom were those he considered lowest, or least developed, such as worms. Above them were things he considered higher, or more developed, such as fish, then birds, then mammals.

For centuries after Aristotle, taxonomy made little progress. People who studied nature tended to group organisms together by obvious features, such as separating trees from grasses or birds from fish. However, they did not try to develop a system for classifying all life. Then, between 1682 and 1705, an English naturalist named John Ray published a plan of the living world that was designed to have a place for every species of plant and animal. Ray's system was hierarchical, with several levels of larger and smaller categories. It was the foundation of modern taxonomy.

Swedish naturalist Carolus Linnaeus (1707–1778) built on that foundation to create the taxonomic system used today. Linnaeus was chiefly interested in plants, but his system of classification included all living things. The highest level of classification was the kingdom. To Linnaeus, everything belonged to either the plant or the animal kingdom. Each of these kingdoms was divided into a number of smaller categories called classes. Each

Calvatia gigantea, the giant puffball, pops up in North American forests in late summer.

class was divided into orders. Each order was divided into genera. Each genus (the singular form of genera) contained one or more species.

Linnaeus also developed another of Ray's ideas, a method for naming species. Before Linnaeus published his important work *System of Nature* in 1735, scientists had no recognized system for referring to plants and animals. Organisms were generally known by their common names, but many of them had different names in various countries. As a result, naturalists often called the same plant or animal by various names—or used the same name for different organisms. Linnaeus wanted to end such confusion, so that scholars everywhere could communicate clearly when writing about plants and animals. He established the practice of giving each plant or animal a two-part scientific name consisting of its genus and species. These names were in Latin, the scientific language of Linnaeus's day. For example, the fungus commonly known as the giant puffball has the scientific name *Calvatia gigantea* or *C. gigantea* after the first time the full name is used. This fungus belongs to the genus *Calvatia,* which includes other kinds of puffballs. The second part of the name, *gigantea,* refers only to the giant puffball.

Linnaeus named hundreds of species. Other scientists quickly adopted his highly flexible system to name many more. The Linnaean system appeared at a time when European naturalists were exploring the rest of the world, finding thousands of new plants and animals. This flood of discoveries was overwhelming at times, but Linnaean taxonomy helped scientists identify and organize their finds for systematic study.

TAXONOMY TODAY

Biologists still use the system of scientific naming that Linnaeus developed (anyone who discovers a new species can choose its scientific name, which is in Latin). Other aspects of taxonomy, though, have changed since Linnaeus's time.

The Taxonomy of the Death Cap

The world's deadliest mushrooms belong to the genus *Amanita,* which contains hundreds of species around the world. Some *Amanita* species are wholesome and delicious—*Amanita caesarea,* for example, got its name because it was a favorite dish of the Roman emperors known as the Caesars. But other species are highly toxic to humans (although squirrels and mice can safely nibble at some of them). Known by such names as destroying angel and fool's mushroom, the toxic members of the *Amanita* genus are responsible for most deaths from mushroom poisoning.

As many as 50 percent of all mushroom poisonings may be caused by one notorious species, *Amanita phalloides,* or the death cap. Just half of one death cap usually contains enough of the toxic compound alpha-amanitin to kill an average-sized adult. *Amanita phalloides* has a history of destruction. One of its most famous victims was Pope Clement VII, who died in Rome in 1534 after eating a death cap. These mushrooms are especially dangerous because they look like other species that are safe to eat.

Here's how the system of taxonomic classification applies to the death cap mushroom:

Kingdom	Fungi (organisms with non-moving bodies made of filaments or budding yeast cells, which digest their food outside their bodies)
Phylum	Basidiomycota (fungi that produce spores on club-shaped cells)
Class	Hymenomycetes (mushrooms, yeasts, and jelly fungi)
Order	Agaricales (most of the gilled mushrooms)
Family	Amanitaceae (several genera of gilled mushrooms, usually found in forests)
Genus	*Amanita* (many species worldwide)
Species	*phalloides* (the death cap)

A person who eats a death cap mushroom quickly suffers violent illness. Then the victim may seem to recover—only to die a day or so later from kidney and liver failure, unless medical treatment started soon after the mushroom was eaten.

As biologists learned more about living things, they added new levels to taxonomy to reflect their growing understanding of the similarities and differences among organisms. Eventually, an organism's full classification could include the following taxonomic levels: kingdom, subkingdom, phylum (some biologists use division instead of phylum for plants and fungi), subphylum, superclass, class, subclass, infraclass, order, superfamily, family, genus, species, and subspecies or variety.

Another change concerned the kinds of information that scientists use to classify organisms. The earliest naturalists used obvious physical features, such as the differences between toadstools and oak trees, to divide organisms into groups. By the time of Ray and Linnaeus, naturalists could study specimens in more detail. Aided by new tools such as the microscope, they explored the inner structures of plants and animals. For a long time after Linnaeus, classification was based mainly on details of anatomy, or physical structure, although scientists also looked at how an organism reproduced and how and where it lived.

Today, biologists can peer more deeply into an organism's inner workings than Aristotle or Linnaeus ever dreamed possible. They can look inside its individual cells and study the arrangement of DNA that makes up its genetic blueprint. Genetic information is key to modern classification because DNA is more than an organism's blueprint—it also reveals how closely that organism is related to other species and how long ago those species separated during the process of evolution.

In recent years, many biologists have pointed out that the Linnaean system is a patchwork of old and new ideas. It doesn't clearly reflect the latest knowledge about the evolutionary links among organisms both living and extinct. Some scientists now call for a new approach to taxonomy, one that is based entirely on evolutionary relationships. One of the most useful new approaches is called phylogenetics, the study of organisms' evolutionary histories. Using a set of organizing steps called cladistics, scientists group together all organisms that are descended from the same ancestor. The result is branching, treelike diagrams called cladograms.

They show the order in which groups of plants or animals split off from a line of shared ancestry.

Although none of the proposed new systems of classifying living things has been adopted by all scientists, the move toward a phylogenetic approach is under way. Most experts recognize the importance of cladistics while still using the two main features of Linnaean taxonomy: the hierarchy of categories and the two-part species name. Yet scientists may disagree about the proper term for a category, or about how to classify a particular plant or animal. Because scientists create and use classifications to suit a variety of purposes, there is no single "right" way to classify organisms.

Even at the highest level of classification, scientists take different approaches to taxonomy. A few of them still divide all life into two kingdoms: plants and animals. At the other extreme are scientists who divide life into thirteen or more kingdoms. Many now group the kingdoms into larger categories called domains or superkingdoms. Most scientists, though, use classification systems with five to seven kingdoms: plants, animals, fungi, and several kingdoms of microscopic organisms such as bacteria, amoebas, and algae.

The classification of living things is always changing, as scientists learn more about the links and differences among organisms. Today, the fungus kingdom is one of the most changeable areas in taxonomy. Traditional categories are giving way to new groupings, mostly based on DNA studies, and several different taxonomies have been suggested. But although scientists may disagree about how to classify mushrooms and their relatives, they agree on one thing: the large and diverse kingdom of the fungi has many secrets still to reveal.

THE FIVE

Many scientists divide Earth's

P9-DHI-866

The
Fungus
Kingdom

KINGDOMS

life-forms into five kingdoms.

PLANTAE

pitcher plants

PROTOCTISTA

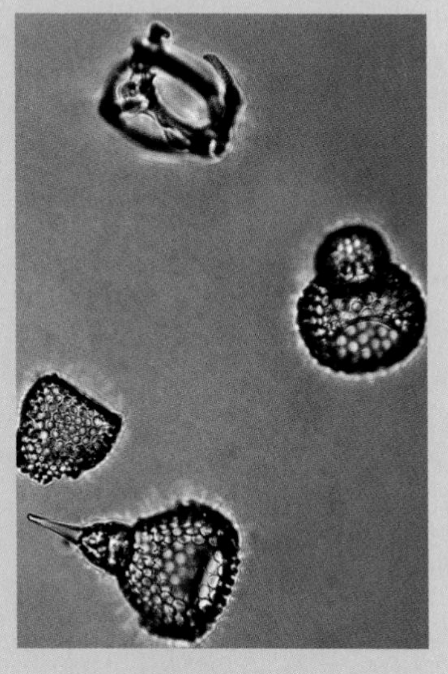

radiolarians

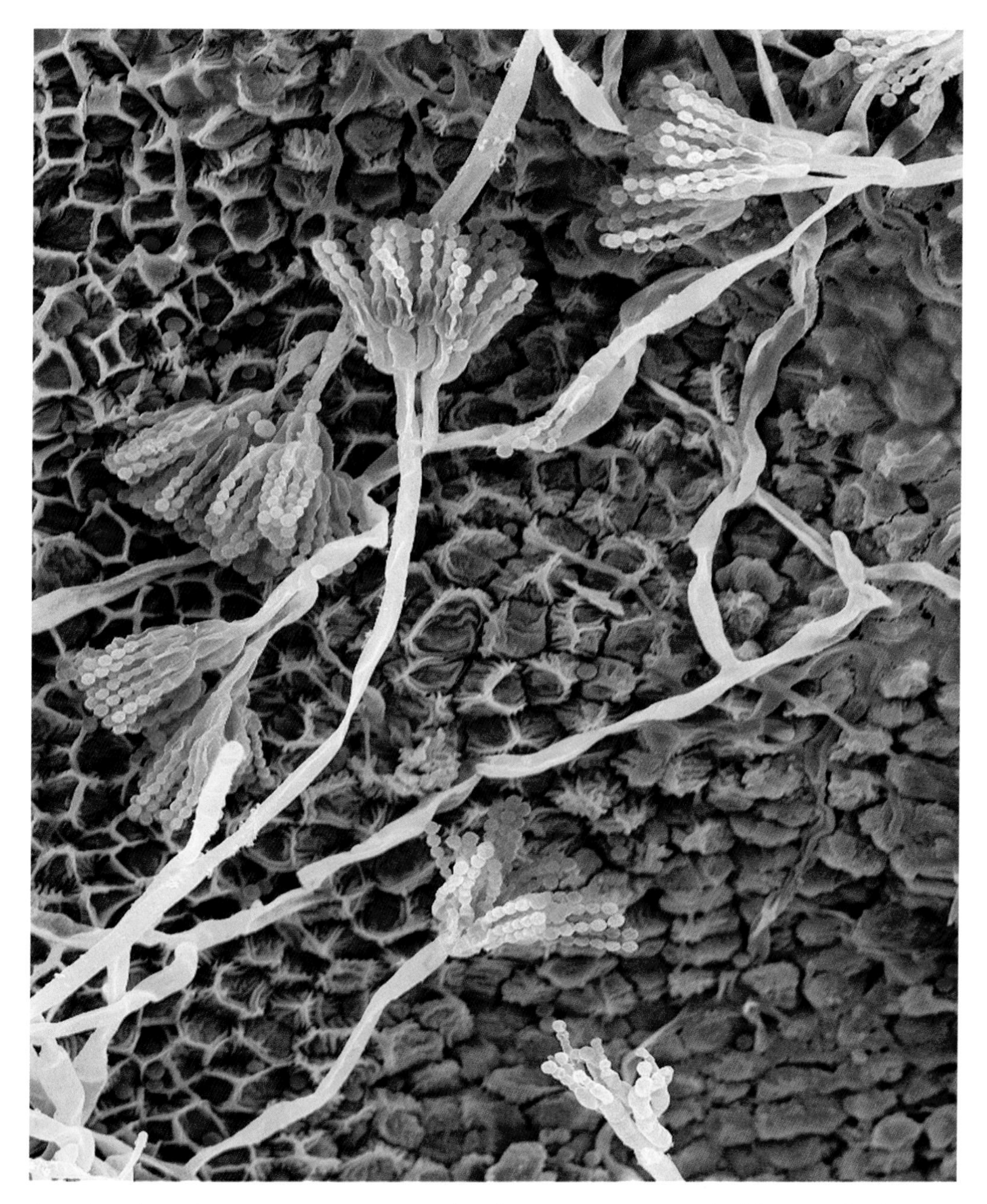

Seen through an electron microscope, a *Penicillium* fungus appears as a web of fine strands. The flowerlike clusters are bunches of spores, its reproductive cells.

CHAPTER **ONE**

A Kingdom of Their Own

Fungi have been around for more than half a billion years. Like all life, they began in the sea. Some kinds of fungi stayed in the water. Their descendants still live in the world's oceans, lakes, and rivers. Other ancient fungi colonized the land and evolved into many forms. Scientists used to call fungi "primitive plants." But although fungi arose very early in the history of life on Earth, there is nothing primitive about this varied and successful group of organisms.

More than 81,000 species of fungi have been named and scientifically described. Each year scientists identify a thousand or so new species. No one knows how many fungi species there are, but in the 1990s mycologist David L. Hawksworth made an estimate.

Hawksworth started with the numbers of known fungus and plant species in the British Isles, where both groups have been well studied. He found that for every known plant species there were six fungus species. Because plants and fungi live in close association everywhere, Hawksworth figured that the 1-to-6 ratio was likely to be about the same around the world. So he multiplied the number of known plant species in the world by six and came up with a figure of 1.65 million fungus species. Some researchers think that the total may be even higher. Whatever the true total may be, the great majority of fungi have not yet been discovered.

FOSSIL FUNGI

The Rhynie chert is a layer of rock in northern Scotland. Chert, a fine-grained quartz, is a excellent preserver of fossils, and the Rhynie chert is famous for beds of fossils that date from the Devonian period, between 360 and 408 million years ago. At that time, the land mass that is now cool, craggy northern Scotland was a tropical flatland of grasses and pools near the equator. Organisms that died there were covered with sand. Over time, they turned to stone.

Some of those organisms were fungi. Fossils from the Rhynie chert suggest that one type of Devonian fungus was a parasite that invaded the cells of aquatic algae. Other Rhynie fungi lived in the stems of land plants. These fossils tell mycologists that as long ago as Devonian times, fungi and plants had already formed feeding partnerships much like the relationships between fungi and plants today. Devonian fossil beds also reveal that by 360 million years ago, before animals with

Rhynie chert is a layer of quartz that contains fossils of several kinds of ancient fungi.

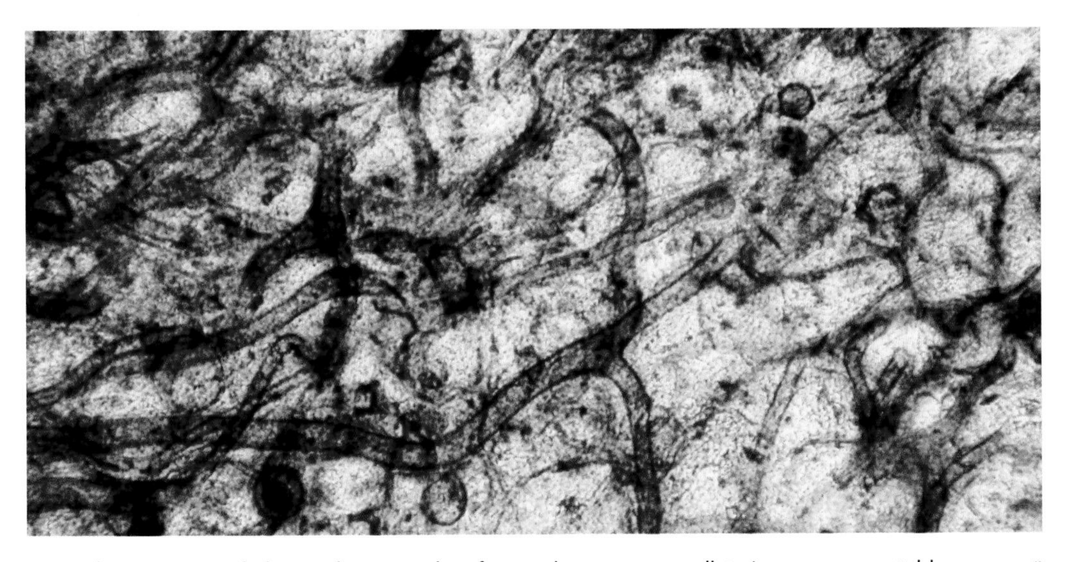

Magnifying a piece of Rhynie chert reveals a fungus that scientists call *Palaeomyces,* or "old musroom." Various *Palaeomyces* species exist in fossil form.

backbones had begun migrating from the sea to the land, the ancestors of the major groups of modern fungi had evolved.

Fungi existed before the Devonian period, but fossils from those earlier times are rare. The oldest that have yet been found come from the Vendian period, which ended 543 million years ago. These fossils were discovered in northern Russia. They resemble a group of modern fungi called the chytrids. Like most fossil fungi, they are very small. The most common kind of fungal fossils, in fact, are spores—the tiny structures that spread the the reproductive material of fungi. Spores at least 570 million years old have been found in Vendian fossil beds.

Fossils of complete mushrooms are rare, but they do exist. Some of the best specimens were found in New Jersey. These small mushrooms were preserved in amber, the hardened sap of trees. They are 90 to 94 million years old. Although they lived during the age of the dinosaurs, these mushrooms are so much like modern species that mycologists can identify them at a glance.

A fifteen- to twenty-million-year old agaric mushroom in amber from the Dominican Republic. Several ancient agaric species have turned up in the Caribbean nation's amber mines.

KINGDOMS AND DOMAINS

It's easy to see why people grouped fungi with plants for most of human history. Like plants, fungi are rooted to the ground, and some of them can be used as food. When Carolus Linnaeus introduced his grand scheme of taxonomy in 1735, he included fungi in the plant kingdom, although modern scientists know that fungi are more closely related to animals. Already in Linnaeus's time, however, a scientific revolution was under way.

Since the mid-seventeenth century, people had been using magnifying lenses to study the natural world. Microscopes opened a window onto an amazing, utterly unexpected realm. Peering through these instruments, people found that living things are made up of tiny structural units, or cells. They discovered that plant cells and fungus cells are very different. Plants contain chlorophyll, a green chemical that lets plants create their own food out of sunlight, air, and water through the process called photosynthesis. Fungi have no chlorophyll and cannot make food through photosynthesis. In addition, their cells do not form the roots, stems, and leaves that are found in most plants. Since ancient times, people had divided all life into plants and animals, but in 1784 scientists agreed to add a third kingdom: the fungi.

The twentieth century brought more changes to taxonomy. Ever since Anton van Leeuwenhoek of Holland made his first microscope in 1665, researchers had been identifying very small living things, mostly invisible to the naked eye, in the water, the air, and all parts of the world. Each of these microscopic organisms had been assigned to either the plant, the animal, or the fungus kingdom, but some of them—such as the bacteria—didn't seem to fit neatly into any category.

By the late 1960s the three-kingdom system no longer seemed adequate. Scientists gradually adopted a new taxonomy with five kingdoms. These were the monerans (bacteria and other single-celled organisms without nuclei, or defined centers, in their cells); the protoctist (small single-celled or simple multicelled organisms with cell nuclei); the fungi; the

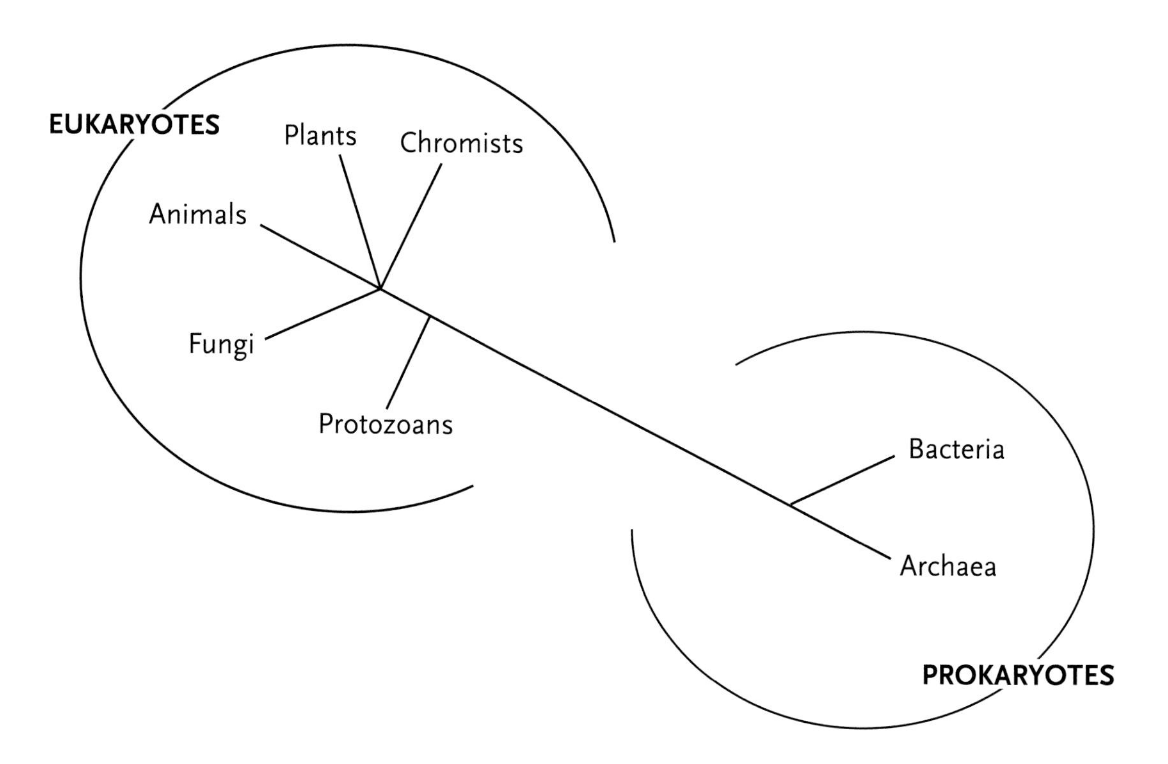

One view of life divides living things into two domains, the prokaryotes and the eukaryotes. The cell of a prokaryote does not have a nucleus (a defined body in the center of the cell), while the cell of a eukaryote has a nucleus and perhaps other specialized bodies. Many scientists recognize two kingdoms of prokaryotes, or monerans: Archaea, an ancient group of bacteria, and Bacteria, which developed later. The eukaryotes can be divided into five kingdoms. One of them is the fungi.

plants; and the animals. This system was linked to an idea about how the different groups evolved from one another. Protoctists evolved from monerans, and then fungi, plants, and animals evolved from protists.

Since that time, some scientists have split the monerans and protoctists into multiple kingdoms. In addition, a new upper level of taxonomy, the domain, has been gaining acceptance. According to this view, all life is divided into two domains. Each domain contains one or more kingdoms, which evolved independently from each other. The fungus kingdom falls into the domain of the eukaryotes, or organisms with cell nuclei.

MAJOR GROUPS OF FUNGI

One of the most widely used systems of taxonomy for the fungi divides the fungus kingdom into six categories. Four of them are phyla (these are sometimes called by an older term, divisions). Each phylum is set apart from the others by small but significant differences in the structures that the fungi use for sexual reproduction. All of the classes, orders, families, genera, and species within a phylum are believed to share a common ancestor.

The other two categories within the fungus kingdom are informal groups: the lichens and the imperfect fungi. Unlike the phyla, these two informal groups contain fungi that are not necessarily related to each other or to any of the formal groups.

Chytridiomycota

The phylum Chytridiomycota contains the chytrids. These small fungi closely resemble the oldest known fossil fungi from the Vendian period. Scientists think that the chytrids were probably the first group of fungi to develop. The chytrid species that exist today have ancestral features not found in the phyla that appeared later.

Chytrids can often be found in soil, but many of them live in salt or fresh water. One unique chytrid feature reflects this water-dwelling way of life. The chytrids' gametes, or sexual reproductive cells, have flagellae. These are whiplike extensions of the cells that lash back and forth in reaction to chemical processes inside the cells. As a result, the chytrids' gametes can swim. No other fungi have reproductive cells with flagellae. That feature, it seems, disappeared from the groups that evolved on land.

Most chytrids live on dead and decaying water plants, but some are found inside live plants or other fungi. A small number of chytrids infect animals. One of these species is responsible for chytridiomycosis, an infectious fungal disease that is attacking frog populations in many parts of the world. It has driven some frog species to extinction. Scientists think that climate change may be making frogs more vulnerable to this fungal disease.

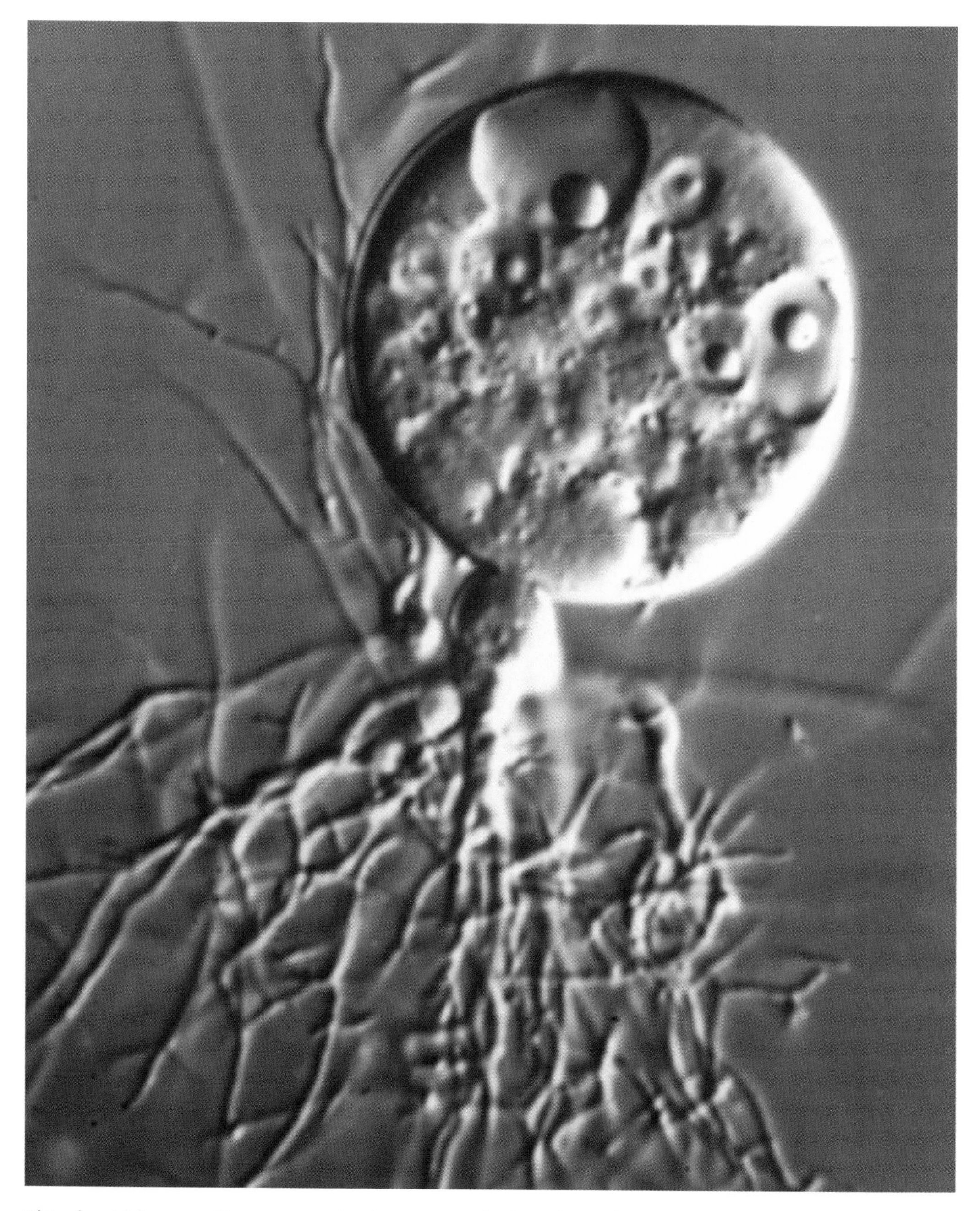

This chytrid fungus, *Chytriomyces hyalinus,* is usually found in soil. It occurs in many parts of the world.

Zygomycota

The phylum Zygomycota contains some fungi that many people would find all too familiar. These fungi are the bread molds, sugar molds, and pin molds—furry-looking fungi that seem to appear out of nowhere on bread, fruit, and other organic matter that contains a lot of sugar. Some of these molds grow very quickly. Delicious red strawberries can turn into disgusting bluish-white blobs overnight. Not all of the Zygomycota live on fruit, however. Other members of this phylum are found in soil, feces, the roots of trees, and the insides of insects.

Many of the Zygomycota are harmless, or even beneficial. *Rhizopus oligosporus,* for example, is used in making tempeh, an Asian food that is a

Tomatoes have fallen victim to a fungus from the Zygomycota group, which includes many fast-growing molds that grow on foods.

form of soy protein. On the other hand, *Rhizopus stolonifer*, in the same genus, is the fungus that spoils strawberries. Most Zygomycota, though, are never noticed by anyone but dedicated mycologists.

The taxonomy of fungi within the Zygomycota phylum is undecided. Some mycologists divide the phylum into two classes. Others identify as many as seven classes. Members of the Zygomycota come and go as scientists revise their ideas. For example, one group of Zygomycota consists of fungi that live in the roots of a wide variety of plants, including cereal grasses and tropical trees. Some taxonomists have promoted this group to the level of a phylum, with the name Glomeromycota. At the same time, the microsporidia, tiny organisms that can cause life-threatening diseases in people, were traditionally considered protists, but some researchers now include them in this group of fungi.

Ascomycota

The phylum Ascomycota includes about three-fourths of all known species of fungi. All of the species in this phylum form reproductive spores inside special cells called asci. The asci are shaped like tiny sacs, which is why members of this phylum are sometimes called sac fungi. The majority of Ascomycota species are very small, even microscopic, but the phylum also includes some larger fungi, such as the elf cups.

The yeast that people have used for thousands of years in brewing beer and making bread belongs in the Ascomycota phylum. So do the large edible mushrooms called morels and the edible underground fungi called truffles. The source of the life-saving drug penicillin is in this phylum, along with the fungus that produces the cancer-causing compound aflatoxin, found in infected nuts and grains.

Fungi in this phylum play a big role in turning dead plant matter into reusable chemical compounds, but they don't stop there. Under the right conditions of temperature and moisture, some Ascomycota will eat wall paint or even jet fuel, because these substances contain carbon compounds that the fungi can digest.

The scarlet elf cap, sometimes called the blood cup, is common in western Europe and parts of North America. This member of the Ascomycota group is most often found growing in dead wood that is covered with damp moss.

The Ascomycota phylum is represented on every continent. Some species are widespread, but others have a very limited geographic distribution. One of the most prized fungi in the world is *Tuber magnatum,* the white Piedmont truffle. It grows in a small region in northern Italy. This fungus is so rare and expensive that simply grating one over a plate of pasta can triple the cost of a meal.

Basidiomycota

In fungi of the phylum Basidiomycota, spores develop on the surface of distinctive cells shaped like bowling pins, or clubs (*basidium* is the Latin word for "club"). Members of this phylum are sometimes called the club fungi. They are a varied group that includes some yeasts, some water-dwelling fungi, and many of the smuts and rusts that attack plants.

Nearly all of the larger fungi are also found in the Badisiomycota phylum. These are the fungi that even people who are not mycologists can recognize—mushrooms, toadstools, puffballs, shelf or bracket fungi, and jelly fungi, which have a moist, shiny surface (wood ear and witches' butter are examples of jelly fungi).

Jelly fungi have slick, moist-looking surfaces. When dried, they become hard, but a soaking in water restores their jellylike appearance.

Lichens

Lichens are found in most parts of the world. Some of them, such as old man's beard, hang from tree branches. Others grow in thin, scalelike layers across rocks. Reindeer moss (also called caribou moss) is a lichen that grows in puffy clumps on the ground. More than 20,000 kinds of lichens are known.

A lichen is not a single organism or even a single species. It is a union of a fungus and an alga growing together in the kind of partnership that biologists call symbiosis, which benefits both partners. The fungus shares the food that the alga makes through photosynthesis. The alga is protected by living inside the fungus, which also provides it with minerals and water. Some lichens contain more than one type of algae, or perhaps blue-green bacteria, which also make food through photosynthesis.

Fungi that live in this kind of symbiosis with algae or photosynthetic bacteria are called lichenized fungi. Scientists think that the relationship between fungi and algae evolved more than once because lichenized fungi are found among unrelated families in two phyla, the sac fungi and the club fungi.

Some of the fungus species that form lichens can also survive on their own, although the fungal form and the lichenized form look different.

A lichen called old man's beard hangs from a beech tree in New Zealand's Kahurangi National Park.

Other lichenized fungi have become dependent on their algal partners and do not live on their own.

One of the first researchers to recognize the true nature of lichens was an Englishwoman named Beatrix Potter, an enthusiastic amateur mycologist who made detailed studies and drawings of fungi and lichens. In the 1890s Potter tried to present her ideas about lichens (and also about molds) to the scientific community, which was dominated by men at that time. Because she was a woman, the scientists did not take her seriously, so she turned her attention to writing children's books about Peter Rabbit and other forest creatures. Potter's tales, with illustrations that include highly accurate pictures of fungi and lichens, have been much loved for more than a century.

A flat, scaly patch of color on rock is one of the most common forms of lichen.

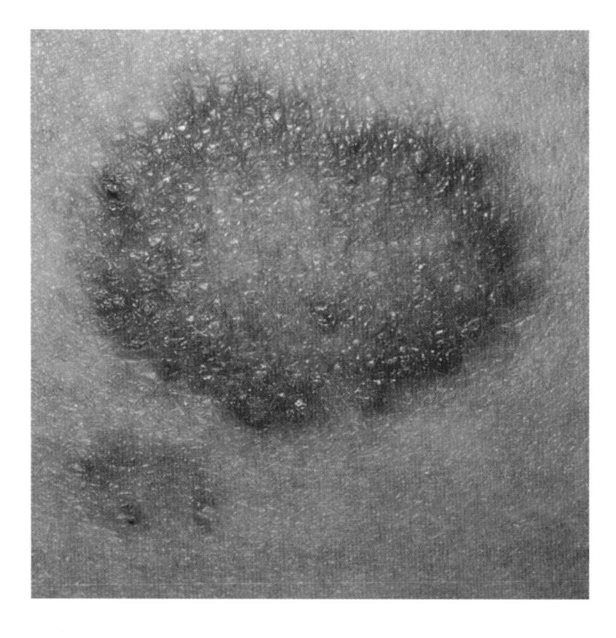

Ringworm is a common and highly contagious fungal infection that may be caused by several kinds of imperfect fungi. It often spreads from pets to people.

Imperfect Fungi

The imperfect fungi are species of club and sac fungi that do not form cells for sexual reproduction. They have lost the ability to reproduce through the union of sex cells, although they can reproduce in other ways. These fungi used to be grouped into a phylum under the name Deuteromycota, but most mycologists no longer consider them a phylum because they do not share a common ancestor. The informal category of imperfect fungi is something like a catch-all drawer for these species until their biology is better understood. In recent years, some researchers have begun moving the imperfect fungi into the Ascomycota and Basidiomycota phyla based on DNA studies that show relationships to fungi in those phyla.

FORMERLY FUNGI

Slime molds and water molds used to be considered fungi. Lately they have been kicked out of the fungus kingdom—by many taxonomists, at least.

Slime molds resemble fungi in certain ways. For example, they produce spores for reproduction. But although slime molds were considered for a long time to be fungi, many experts now think that they make up several different categories of eukaryotic life. Not only are slime molds not closely related to the fungi, but the different kinds of slime molds are not even closely related to each other.

Water molds also have some resemblances to fungi. They feed on dead and decaying plant matter, and they grow in the form of threadlike filaments. Traditionally, water molds were considered to be a phylum of the fungus kingdom, under the name Oomycota. Now, however, some scientists place them in a suggested new kingdom called Chromista (some taxonomists call this kingdom Stramenopila). It includes photosynthetic organisms such as tiny diatoms, giant kelp and other brown algae, and some mildews.

Some mycologists question whether the water molds should be removed from the fungus kingdom. Although the cell walls of water molds are made of a combination of materials found only in the other chromists, not in the true fungi, the water molds look and act a lot like true fungi. They also cause plant and animal diseases like the diseases that true fungi cause. Research into these diseases—and how to cure or prevent them—continues without much concern for the shifting boundaries of kingdoms and phyla.

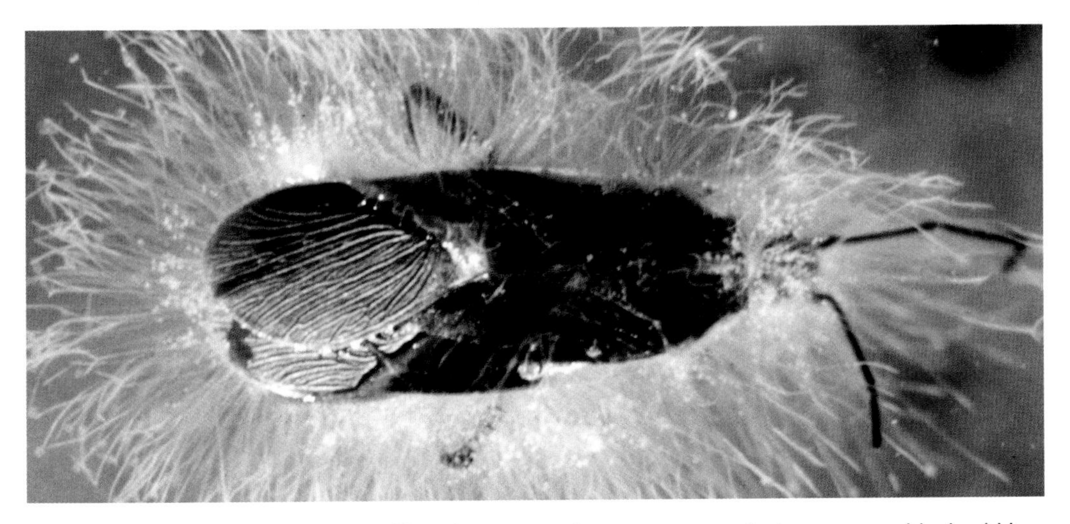

Water mold has infected an insect. Although scientists do not agree on whether water molds should be classified with the fungi, these molds act much like fungi.

The Mystery of the Giant Mushroom

Did fungal forests tower over the landscape during the Devonian period, from 360 to 408 million years ago? That question is debated by paleobotanists, scientists who study the remains of ancient plants and fungi. At the heart of the debate is a mysterious fossil named *Prototaxites.* The longest known specimen of *Prototaxites* stood at least 29 feet (8.8 m) tall. If it was a mushroom, it was the biggest that ever lived.

A geologist named J.William Dawson made the first scientific description of *Prototaxites* in 1859, based on specimens from the Gaspé Peninsula in Canada. They looked like chunks of fossilized tree trunks, or petrified wood, with visible rings and hollow tubes in their centers. Dawson thought they were the remains of ancient conifers, trees related to present-day evergreens. In the years that followed, other *Prototaxites* fossils turned up around the world. A broken trunk measuring 17.5 feet (5.3 m) long and 4.6 feet (1.4 m) across was found on a beach in Saudi Arabia. The longest fossil came from New York State. Broken chunks of *Prototaxites* have also come to light in fossil beds and stone quarries across northern Europe.

Ever since Dawson announced his discovery, scientists have put forward other theories about *Prototaxites.* They long ago rejected Dawson's idea that the fossils were petrified conifer trunks. Some researchers have called *Prototaxites* an alga, possibly an early relative of today's brown algae, which can reach great lengths in the sea. Others think that *Prototaxites* was a lichen, an organism made up of a fungus and an alga together. In 2001, an American scientist named Francis Hueber published the results of twenty years of studying *Prototaxites.* Hueber claimed that the microscopic structure of the fossils proves that *Prototaxites* was the fruiting body, or mushroom, of an enormous fungus.

The year after Hueber's work appeared, a French scientist named Marc-André Selosse argued that *Prototaxites* should be considered a lichen, not a fungus (although a lichen is part fungus). The nature of this massive, mysterious organism is not yet fully known, but its fossils tell us that it was far larger than the largest plants of its time. *Prototaxites* was the biggest organism living on land in the early Devonian period.

A fossilized chunk of *Prototaxites* shows growth rings like those of tree trunks. This piece came from The Netherlands, where *Prototaxites* fossils have been found during dredging of the canals.

The fly agaric, *Amanita muscaria,* originated in the forests of the northern hemisphere but is now found in many parts of the world. This poisonous, white-spotted fungus is one of the most recognizable mushrooms in works of art.

CHAPTER **TWO**

What Is a Fungus?

When most people think of fungi, they don't picture tiny organisms that can be seen only through a microscope. They picture a mushroom springing from the forest floor, or a flat-topped shelf fungus growing on the side of a tree. These fungal forms have been familiar for thousands of years. People have used them as food or drugs. Still, in some times and places, mushrooms have been feared.

Europeans of the Middle Ages found something suspicious in the way mushrooms often appeared on dead things, such as rotten logs. Mushrooms' rapid growth also seemed unnatural. In addition, people knew that many mushrooms could make them sick, or kill them. The fact that some mushrooms have a pale, corpselike color didn't help their image, nor did the fact that a few mushrooms glow in the dark with an eerie, cold light. For all of these reasons, mushrooms seemed evil or dangerous. People associated them with ghosts or witches.

Glow-in-the-dark mushrooms are no longer seen as ghostly presences. Scientists know that they are examples of bioluminescence, the ability that some organisms have to make light through chemical reactions in their cells. In the old-growth forests of southern Brazil, Dennis Desjardin of San

Looking like a fleet of tiny flying saucers, bioluminescent fungi on the Asian island of New Guinea glow in the darkness of the night forest.

Francisco State University and other researchers recently discovered a bioluminescent fungus they named *Mycena lucentipes,* which means "glowing stem." It is bright enough to read by. Thanks to the work of generations of scientists, folklore and old beliefs about fungi have been replaced by a better understanding of the fungus kingdom. Fungi are unique, different from other organisms in the way they are built and how they live.

FUNGUS FORM

Unlike bacteria and other prokaryotes, fungi are made of cells that contain nuclei, or centers. Fungus cells also have walls, which are found in plant cells but not in animal cells. But unlike plant cells, fungus cells have walls made of chitin, which is the material of the stiff outer shells of insects and spiders. This chitin in a fungus's cell walls acts like a skeleton, supporting the fungus and giving it shape.

A fungus's body is fairly simple. Instead of having different organs or structural parts, the entire body is made up of the same stuff: long, thin cells that join end-to-end to form threadlike, microscopically fine tubes called hyphae. In chytrids and members of the Zygomycota, the cells that make up a hypha run together without cell walls across the tubes. In the sac fungi and club fungi, a cross-wall called a septum marks the boundary between two cells in a hypha.

As a fungus develops, its hyphae branch to form networks. A complete network, cluster, or mat of hyphae is called a mycelium. This mass of filaments is the living body of the fungus. It grows by extending each hypha outward. In this way the mycelium spreads through soil, wood, or other

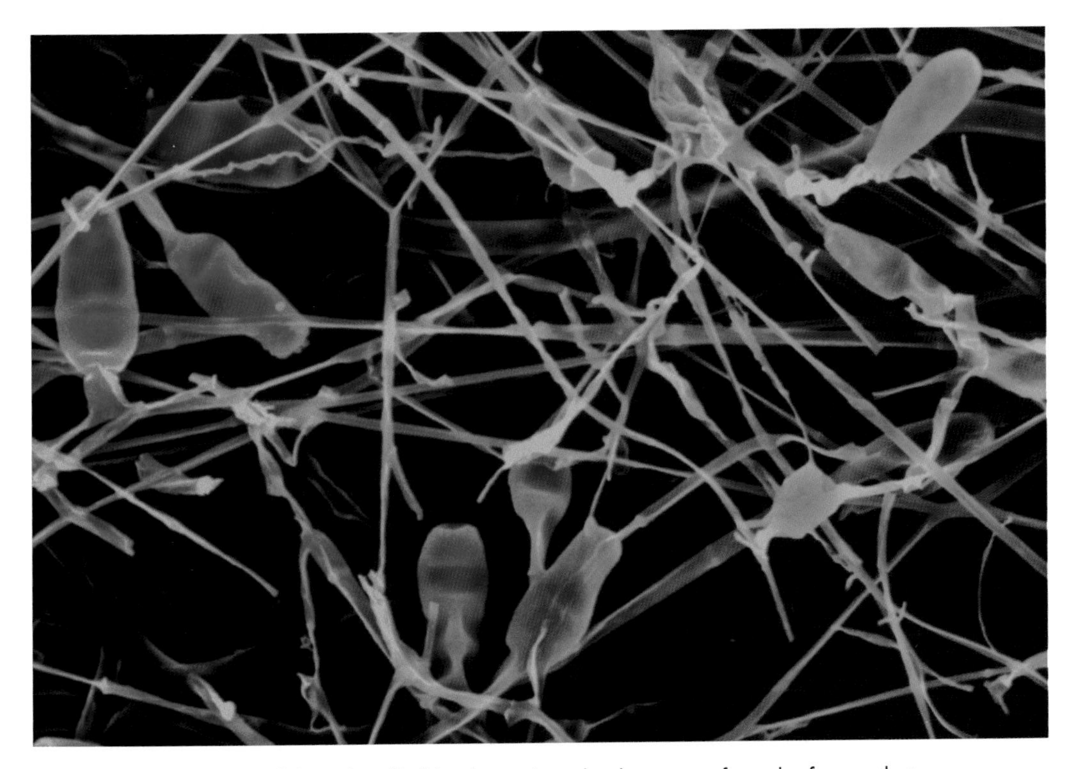

A fungus is a network of threads called hyphae. These hyphae come from the fungus that causes athlete's foot, a skin infection.

BUILDING A MYCELIUM

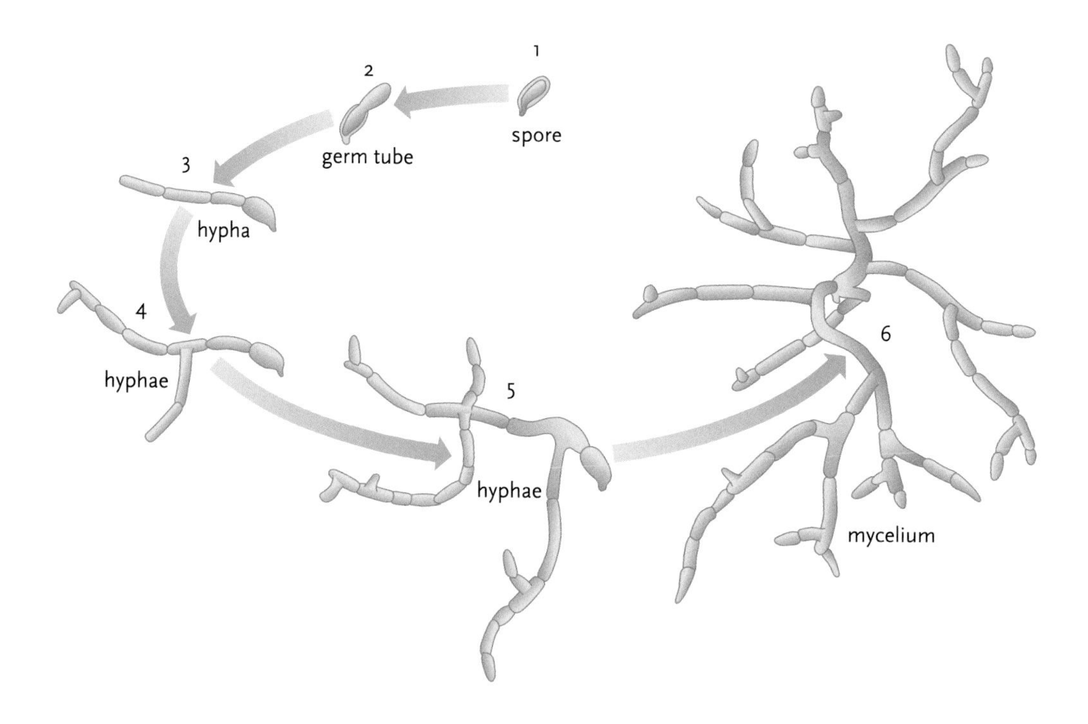

A spore (1) is the reproductive material of a fungus. In favorable conditions, it sprouts (2) and begins growing by adding cells, to form a strand called a hypha (3). As some of the cells branch outward, more hyphae form (4 and 5). They form a mat or web called a mycelium (6). This is the fungus's vegetative body.

matter. Some rain forest species live in the air—clusters of hyphae form sturdy strands that spread along tree branches. These mycelia sometimes form aerial webs or mats that catch falling leaves and twigs.

The mycelium is sometimes called the thallus. It is also known as the vegetative body or vegetative stage of the fungus. Some fungi also have a sporocarp, or fruiting body. A fruiting body is an outgrowth of the mycelium that releases spores. It forms out of the mycelium when conditions are right for sexual reproduction.

Mushrooms are the temporary fruiting bodies of fungi, not the fungi themselves. The real fungi are the mycelia, which may be hidden from view because they are underground or inside a log or other material. In the case of the giant *Armillaria ostoyae* that lives in Oregon's Blue Mountains, the only parts of the fungus that most people see are the clumps of golden-brown mushrooms that rise out of the forest floor in the fall.

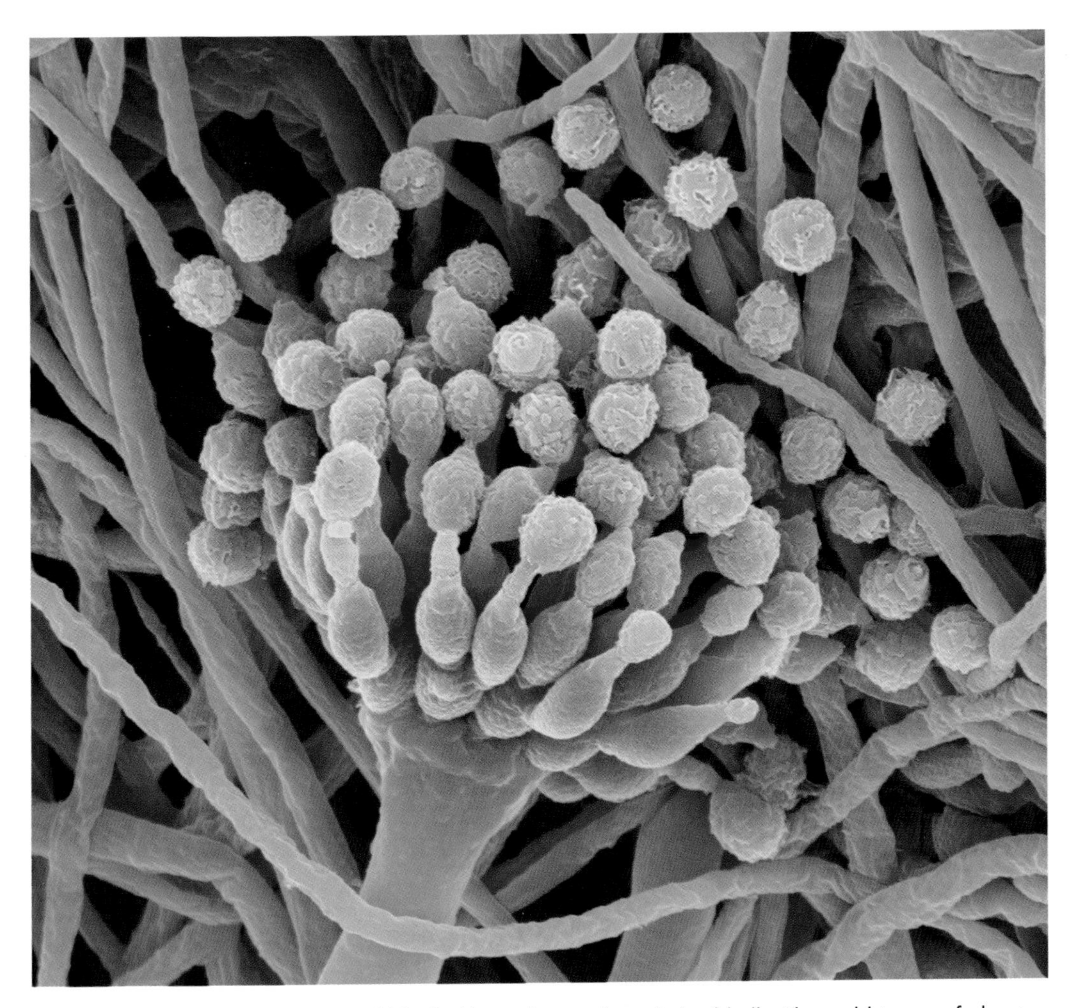

The fruiting body of this green mold looks like a cluster of small dumbbells. The mold is one of about two hundred species in the genus *Aspergillus,* which are found worldwide.

PARTS OF A MUSHROOM

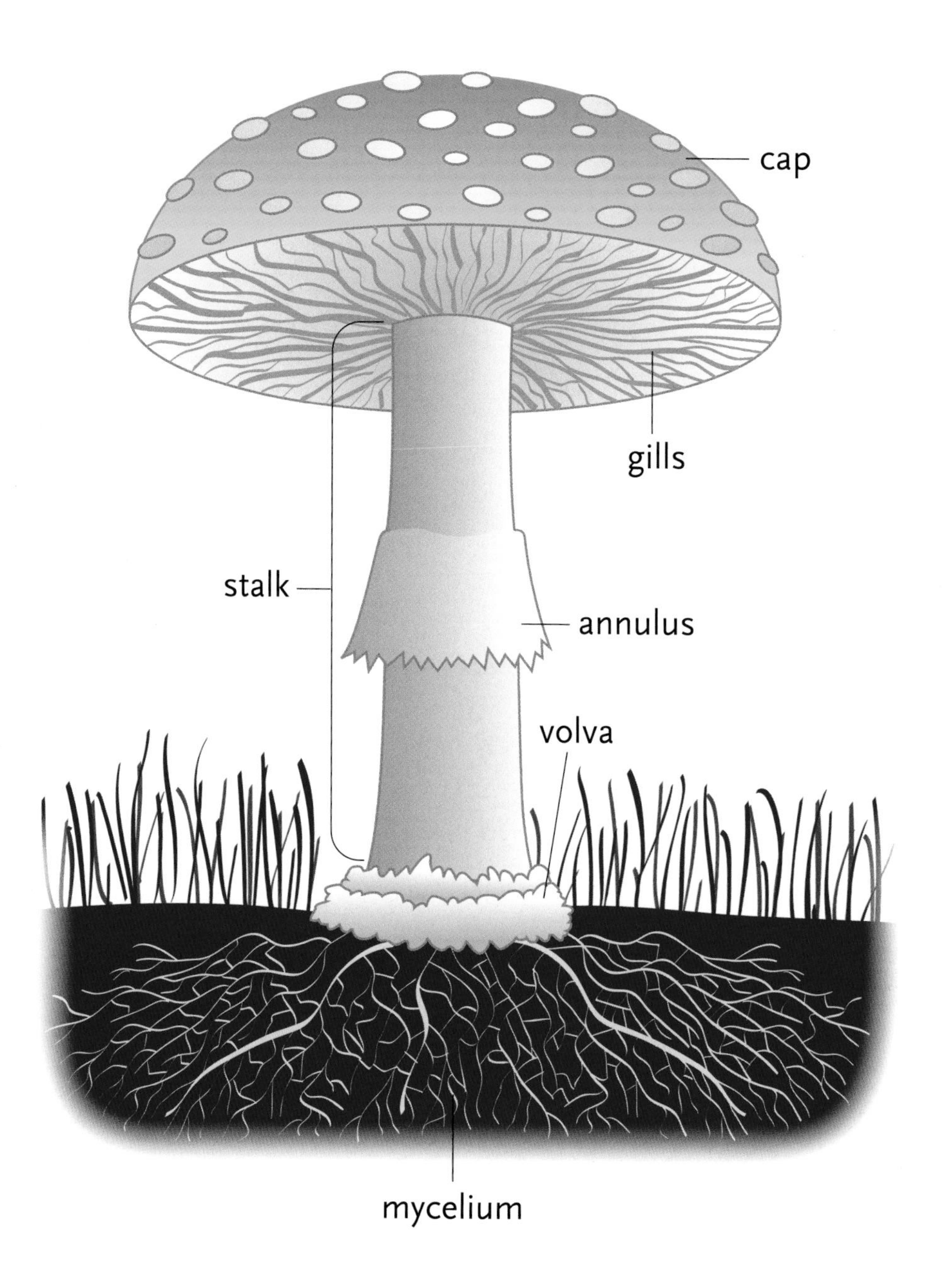

There are many different kinds of fruiting bodies. The umbrella-shaped mushroom—the familiar shape of a cap on top of a stalk—is a gilled mushroom. Its releases its spores from tiny pores, or holes, in its gills, which are thin platelike structures on the underside of the cap. The umbrella-shaped gilled mushrooms are called agarics because most of them belong to an order called Agaricales, in the Basidiomycota phylum. The chanterelles, another kind of gilled mushroom, take a different form. They are shaped like fans, trumpets, or cups. Their gills are folds that run down the length

Gills are visible on the underside of the cap of this porcelain mushroom (also known as the poached-egg mushroom).

The fruiting body of the lacy stinkhorn fungus, found in tropical climates, looks like a net or veil. It is sometimes called the bridal veil mushroom, although it gives off an unpleasant smell that does not seem to go with wedding finery.

of the fruiting body. Oyster mushrooms and split gill fungi also have gills that cover most of the fruiting body below the cap.

Morels, the fruiting bodies of some sac fungi, look like sponges or honeycombs. Truffles resemble lumpy potatoes. Fruiting bodies can also take the form of nets, crusts, spikes, and cups. The common names of many fungi come from the way their fruiting bodies look. Stag's horn, for example, is a yellowish jelly fungus shaped like a set of branching horns. Candle snuff fungus looks like a dark, many-branched candle topped with ashes. Puffballs, earthstars, and earthballs have round, ball-like shapes. Some of these can be huge. The record-holder is a giant puffball that was picked in

Bracket fungi adorn a fallen tree in a German forest. Wood is the ideal home and food for many types of fungi.

Canada in 1987. It measured 8.7 feet (2.6 m) across and weighed 48.5 pounds (22 kilograms).

Shelf or bracket fungi have tubes, not gills, beneath their caps. They release their spores through these tubes. The shelf fungi are often woody or leathery in texture. They may have no stems; instead, they grow right out of trees and logs. Unlike mushrooms, the fruiting bodies of shelf fungi can be perennial, which means that they last for a long time. Each time the fungus produces spores, a new layer of pores develops on the underside of the fruiting body.

HOW FUNGI LIVE

Fungi can live in very dry environments—mushrooms are found in most of the world's deserts—but they still require water, like all living things. They also need food. Fungi are different from plants and animals in the way they get food. Unlike plants, they cannot produce their own food through photosynthesis. Unlike animals, they cannot absorb food by taking it into their bodies and then digesting. Fungi must first digest the food outside their bodies, and then take it in. Some small creatures, such as spiders, also eat this way, but they drink in the digested food as a liquid. Fungi absorb it one molecule at a time.

To digest their food, fungi release enzymes that break plant and animal tissues around the mycelium into simple chemical compounds in liquid form. The mycelium then absorbs these liquids and the nutrients they contain. Unlike plants, which store their food as starches, fungi store it in the form of a chemical called glycogen. Animals also store food in their bodies as glycogen. This is one of several biological features that make some scientists think that fungi have more in common with animals than with plants.

A fungus's food source is whatever the mycelium is growing in—soil, wood, a leaf, skin, or some other material. The material on which a fungus feeds and grows is called its substrate. In the case of *Rhizopus stolonifer,* for example, the substrate is a strawberry. You could say that the fungus eats its home, or that it lives in its food.

FUNGAL REPRODUCTION

Fungi reproduce in a variety of ways, and most of them can reproduce in more than one way, depending on circumstances. Some forms of fungal reproduction are asexual, and others are sexual.

Asexual reproduction occurs when an organism creates a copy of itself using only its own genetic material. It reproduces on its own, without the help of another member of its species. Asexual reproduction gives organisms a way to keep their species going, even if there are no other members of the species around. But asexual reproduction has a disadvantage. It simply copies the same genetic material over and over again. The only changes come from random mutations, so evolution proceeds slowly.

Sexual reproduction occurs when a new organism is created by the blending of genetic material from two parent organisms. In animals and plants that reproduce sexually, the two parent organisms are male and female. Mycologists do not usually use gender terms for fungi, though. Instead, they describe sexual reproduction as the union of two mating cells, or the joining of two mycelia of different mating types.

The same species of fungus can produce individual mycelia of two or more mating types. Having many mating types within a species makes it more likely that a mycelium will encounter another mycelium that is compatible—which means the two are of different mating types and can mate. For sexual reproduction to take place, a hypha from one mycelium must fuse, or join, with a hypha from the other mycelium.

Sexual reproduction gives species an evolutionary advantage. By mixing genes, sexual reproduction creates more chances for mutations to occur, which speeds up evolution. Fungi that reproduce sexually are likely to respond faster than asexual fungi to environmental pressures, such as rising temperatures or the use of pesticides, because each new generation brings more opportunities to develop favorable combinations of genes.

Reproduction is the basis for classifying groups within the fungus kingdom. Each of the four phyla of fungi has its own version of sexual reproduction. In addition, the chytrids, sac fungi, and zygomycotes also reproduce asexually. Most of the club fungi do not reproduce asexually. The informal group called the imperfect fungi can only reproduce asexually.

Asexual Reproduction

Fungi reproduce asexually in various ways, depending upon the species. Some single-celled fungi, such as yeasts, reproduce by budding. This happens when a small outgrowth of a yeast cell grows until it is large enough to live on its own. It splits off as an independent cell. Other yeasts reproduce through fission, when a yeast cell divides into two daughter cells. Cells produced by budding and fission are clones, organisms that are genetically identical to the parent cells.

Other fungi reproduce asexually by producing spores, tiny packets of genetic material that are something like seeds. In the chytrids and zygomycotes, asexual spores form within special structures called sporangia. In the sac fungi and the imperfect fungi, asexual spores develop on the hyphae.

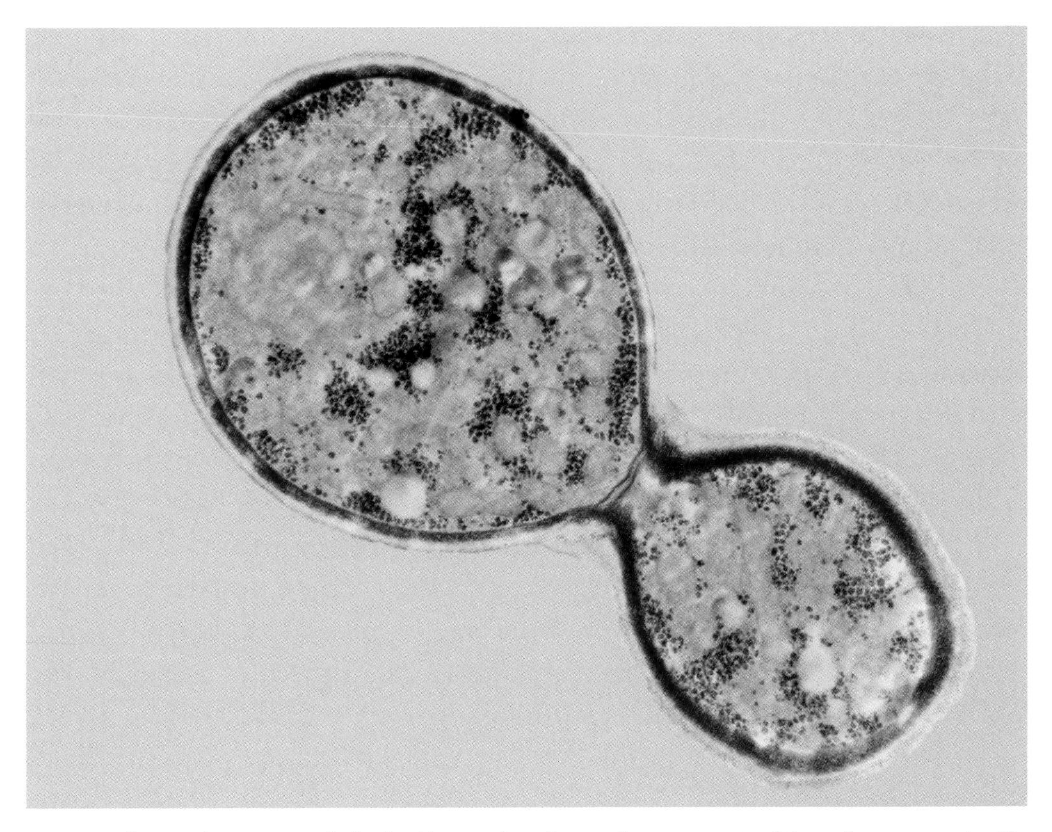

A yeast cell reproduces asexually by budding. When the smaller outgrowth of the cell separates, it will be a new yeast organism.

Each spore carries the genetic material of its parent. If it lands in the right environment, it can germinate and grow into a clone of the parent.

Most fungi can reproduce asexually with spores, but some fungi also reproduce asexually through vegetative growth. This kind of reproduction occurs when a piece of a parent organism can grow into a whole new organism. A broken-off chunk of a mycelium, for example, becomes a new mycelium, with the same genetic makeup as its parent.

Sexual Reproduction

All of the fungi except the imperfect fungi and the Glomeromycota have sexual reproduction as part of their life cycles. The way sexual reproduction takes place, though, differs from phylum to phylum.

In the chytrids, sexual reproduction occurs when two different mating gametes fuse, or combine, to form a zygote that grows into a new chytrid. This organism, in turn, produces spores. Depending on the type of spore, the mycelium that develops from the spore may have either all genetic material from both parent cells or some genetic material from each parent.

The zygomycotes reproduce sexually through a fusion, or merging, of hyphae that contain compatible mating cells—either from the same mycelium or from different mycelia. Their fusion creates a reproductive cell called a zygospore, which germinates into a new mycelium. This mycelium quickly forms a sporangium that produces asexual spores.

In the ascomycotes, or sac fungi, sexual reproduction takes place when different mating types of mycelia join together to form a new mycelium that contains two nuclei of different mating types. This new mycelium produces a fruiting body made of sac-shaped cells, the asci. Within the asci the two nuclei fuse and then divide and produce spores, called ascospores in this phylum. Each ascospore can germinate into a new mycelium that will be able to reproduce both asexually, from its hyphae, and sexually, by joining with a compatible mycelium to form a new fruiting body.

The basidiomycotes, or club fungi, also reproduce sexually through the fusion of compatible mycelia. This results in a new mycelium that

TYPES OF SPORES

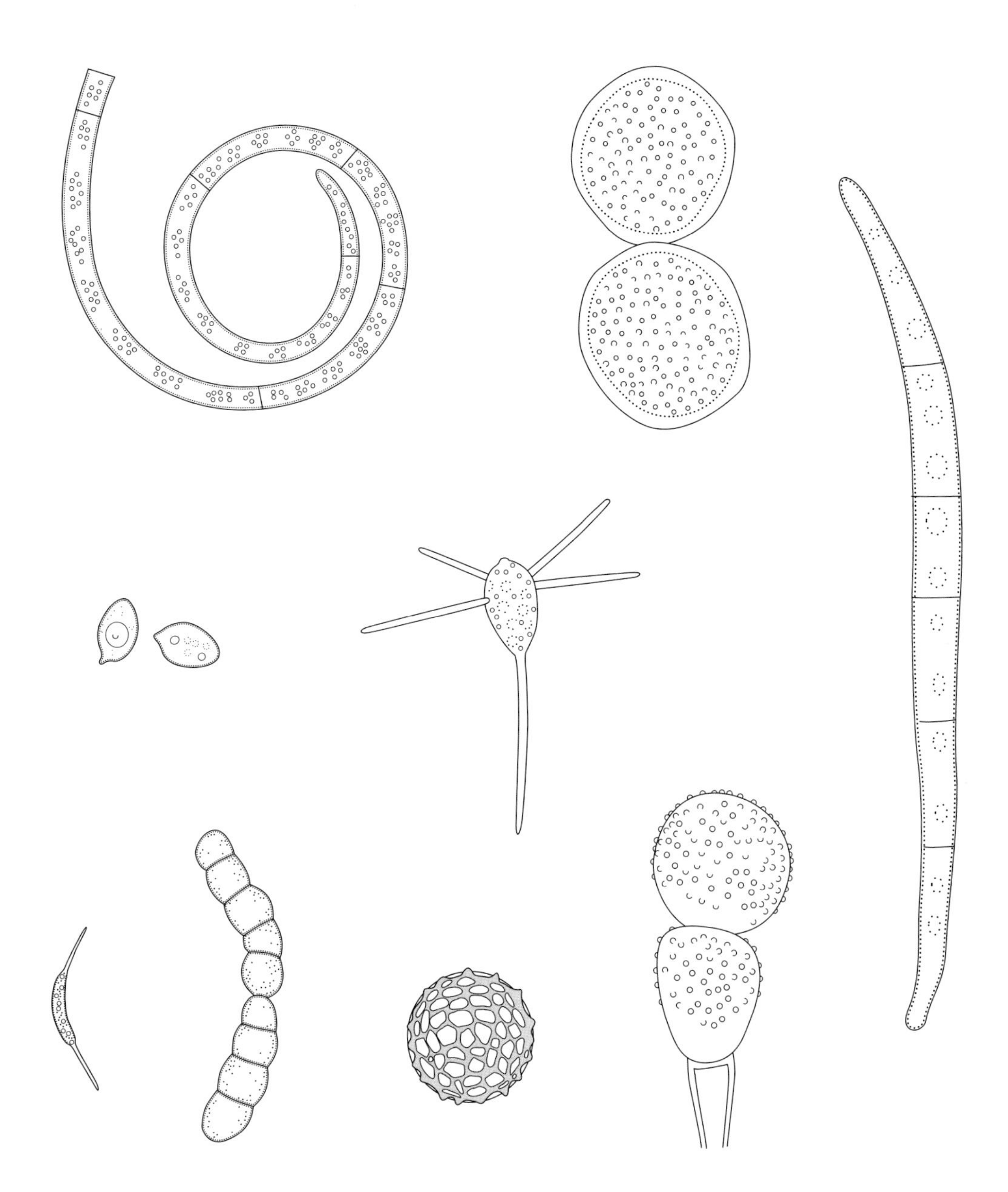

The spores of fungi take many shapes, but all are extremely small. Many spores can travel for long distances on the breeze. Others attach themselves to insects or animals, which spread them to new locations.

The fairy club (also called the upright coral) is produced by *Ramaria stricta,* a fungus often found growing in stumps or woodpiles.

produces a fruiting body with club-shaped cells. Basidiospores, the spores of the club fungi, form on the surface of these cells. Some members of this phylum—the rusts and smuts that live on plants such as cereal grains—can fertilize themselves by fusing compatible hyphae, but they also pass through one or more stages of asexual reproduction during their life cycles.

Spores

All of the fungi except the yeasts produce sexual spores, asexual spores, or both. In order to germinate, these spores must go out into the world and find a welcoming environment—not too hot or cold, not too dry, with a nourishing substrate. Some fungal spores can survive for years until the conditions are right for them to germinate, but they must still reach a suitable location. How do they get there?

The asexual and sexual spores of the chytrids move through water by lashing their flagellae. These are the only fungal spores that move independently. The others must be carried by wind, insects, or animals. In many cases, the spores simply fall or drift off the fruiting bodies. Other

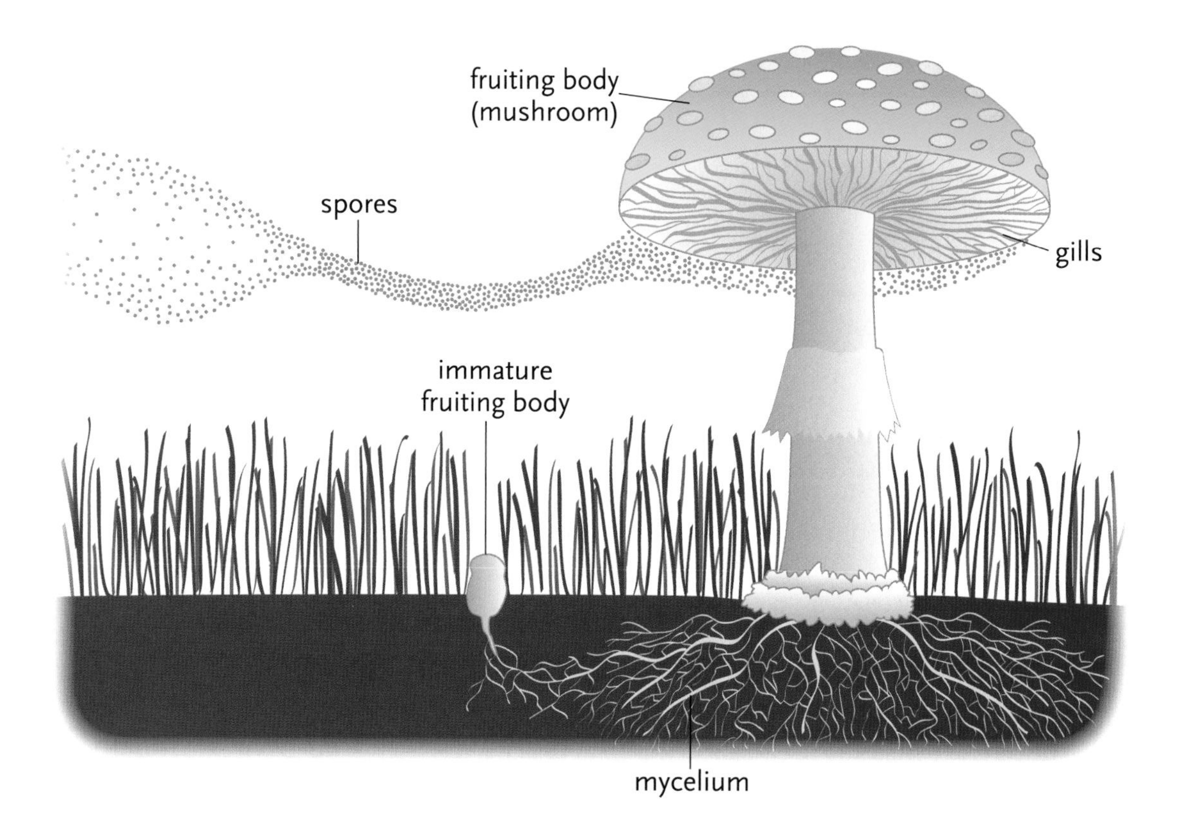

From underground, the mycelium sends out thousands of spores by producing the temporary, above-ground structures that we call mushrooms. A single mycelium can produce many mushrooms. Two are shown here, but some fungi produce hundreds.

species, however, launch their spores into the air with mechanisms that are like biological catapults, activated by water pressure or the weight of the ripened spores.

Some fungi let insects do the work for them. Stinkhorns, for example, produce spores surrounded by a sticky mucus that smells like rotting flesh—an aroma that flies find appetizing. Flies land on the stinkhorns to sample the mucus, and spores stick to the flies. When the insects leave, they spread the spores to new locations.

Bluebottle flies cluster on a starfish stinkhorn in Costa Rica. One scientist has described the stinkhorn's smell as "very ripe roadkill."

Spores come in many colors and a variety of shapes: stars, spirals, boomerangs, and dozens more. They also come in various sizes, but all of them are small. Take a deep breath, especially outdoors in the summer or fall, and the chances are good that you have inhaled some invisible fungal spores. They are often present in the air, which is no surprise—there are a lot of fungi in the world, and some fungi produce a lot of spores. A single giant puffball can release trillions of them. Although most spores are harmless to the majority of people, they can trigger allergic reactions or asthma attacks in some individuals.

Spores fly up from a pair of common puffballs.

One of the ways mushroom collectors identify the species they have found is by making spore prints, letting the spores fall out of the gills or pores onto light and dark paper. This shows the color of the spores, which is often a key to identification. A carefully made spore print, however, also reveals part of the fungus's structure that many people never notice. The gills or pores on the fruiting body can form a delicate tracery on the spore print, the hidden signature of the species.

Toadstools, Death Chairs, and Toads' Tools

What is a toadstool? And did it get its name because toads sit on it?

The first question is easier to answer than the second. The word "toadstool" has no scientific meaning—it is just another word for "mushroom." Some people use it to refer to any kind of mushroom. Others use it only for poisonous mushrooms. In Europe and Great Britain, many people limit the term "toadstool" to a single species of mushroom, *Amanita muscaria,* the fly agaric. Known for its scarlet, white-spotted cap, the fly agaric is poisonous to humans.

The origin of the word "toadstool" is something of a mystery. One explanation for the word is that "stool" is an old name for the cap, or top, of a mushroom. People combined it with "toad" because they believed that toads (members of the frog order of amphibians) were poisonous. Toads and mushroom caps, two things considered dangerous or evil, got lumped together in a single word.

Another explanation is that "toadstool" comes from the German words *tod* (death) and *stuhl* (chair). *Amanita muscaria* might have been called the "death-chair" because it is poisonous and shaped like a one-legged stool, or chair.

A third suggestion is that toads really do lurk near certain mushrooms, such as the fly agaric. The idea is that the toads use the mushrooms as aids to catching food. Insects land on these fungi and absorb chemicals that make them dizzy or confused. This makes it easy for toads to catch the insects, so the toads hang around waiting for quick meals. This theory is unproven, however. Maybe the answer is much simpler—someone once spotted a toad or frog squatting on top of a mushroom, and called the mushroom a toad's stool, and the name stuck.

CHILDREN'S ROOM

Shelf fungi speckle the trunk of a live tree. Unlike softer-bodied, fast-growing ground mushrooms, these slow-growing fungi are hard and woody. They may last for years.

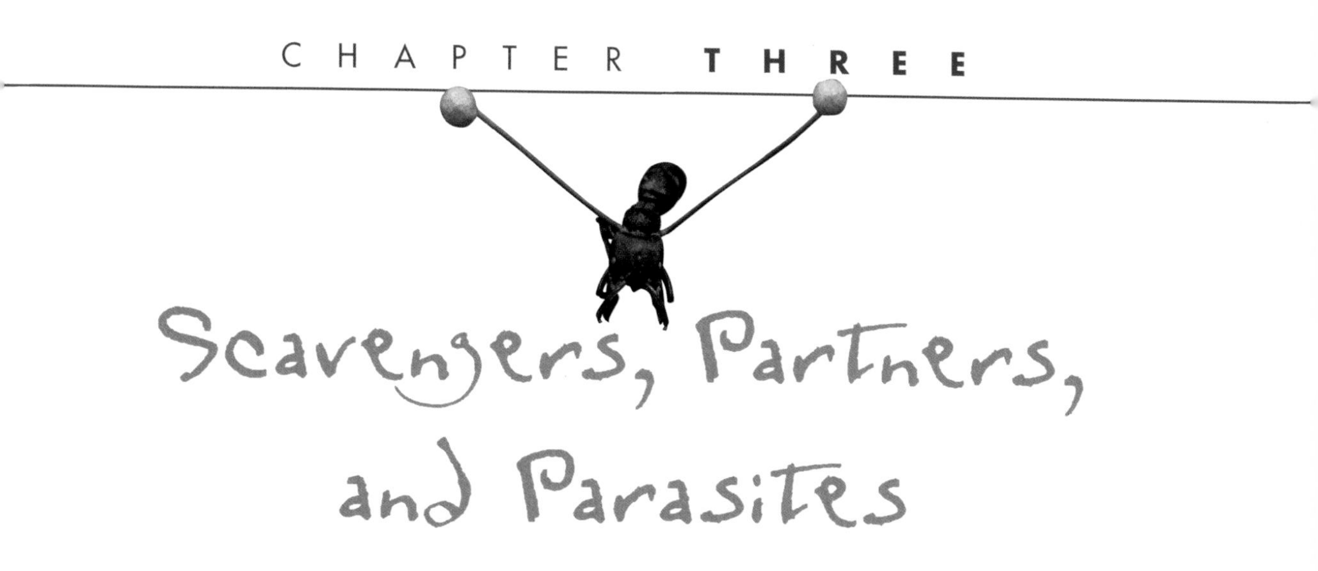

CHAPTER THREE

Scavengers, Partners, and Parasites

In 1620, the Pilgrims crossed the Atlantic from England to Plymouth Rock, Massachusetts. They had a miserable trip, partly because their ship, the *Mayflower,* was overcrowded. There were originally two ships, but everyone had to cram into the *Mayflower* because the *Speedwell* couldn't make the voyage. From descriptions written at the time, it appears that many of the *Speedwell*'s timbers were weak and crumbling, riddled with a condition called dry rot that happens when a fungus feeds on dead wood. In the case of the *Speedwell,* unfortunately for the Pilgrims, the dead wood was not a fallen tree, quietly rotting away in a forest. The wood had been made into a ship, but that did not make it any less appetizing to the fungus.

The fungi that cause dry rot may have originally lived in the Himalaya Mountains of Asia. Over time, they made their way around the world, traveling as spores or carried in infected wood. Human activity helped spread these fungi, which is unfortunate, because from the human point of view, dry rot is highly destructive. It can eat away entire buildings. Despite the "dry" in its name, it flourishes in damp wood with poor air circulation. One reason for its destructive power is that *Serpula lacrymans,* the fungus that causes most cases of dry rot, is very good at finding food. Its hyphae

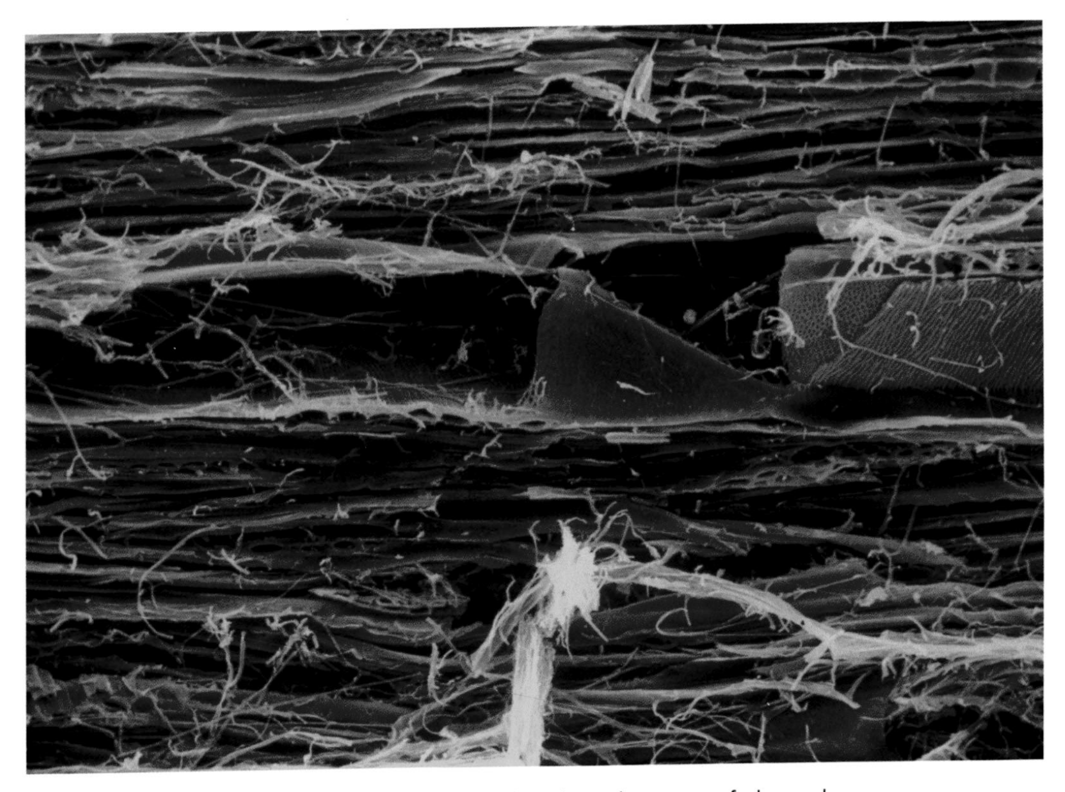

A close-up view of dry rot sending its hungry hyphae through a piece of plywood.

form long, tough strands that probe outward from an infected piece of wood, looking for a new piece of wood to infect, even if they have to grow through yards or meters of concrete or brickwork to reach it.

Not every fungus seeks out food as aggressively as *S. lacrymans,* but fungi are busy everywhere, turning all kinds of matter into chemical soup that they can absorb. Fungi can be sorted into three large groups by their ecological roles: what they eat, and how they interact with the other organisms in their environments. Some fungi are scavengers that break down dead plant and animal matter. Some form partnerships with other organisms that benefit both parties. And some are parasites that feed on living things, weakening or killing their hosts in the process.

THE SCAVENGERS

Life-forms that feed on dead and decaying organic material are decomposers. Scientists sometimes call them saprotrophs, from the Greek words *sapros* (which means "rotten") and *trophe* ("food"). The vultures that devour animals killed on the highways are saprotrophs. So are the mycelia that use organic, or carbon-based, materials as their substrates.

A fungus's substrate doesn't have to be something as obvious as a rotten log or a dead animal. Microfungi can attack glue, insulation, and even the coatings of camera and binocular lenses. Keeping optical equipment free of fungi can be a challenge, especially in the tropics, where fungi thrive in the warmth and moisture.

Trametes versicolor is known in the United States as the turkey tail fungus. This very common fungus is one of the chief decomposers of dead wood.

Fungi are not the only things that decompose dead plant and animal matter. Bacteria and protists are also part of nature's clean-up crew. So are many insects and small animals. Fungi, however, play a key role in turning dead plants and animals into food. They help recycle the energy that is tied up in the planet's food chain. Fungi can break down wood and other complex substances that no other organisms can completely decompose. During their digestion process, fungi break down the complex molecules of dead organic matter into simpler forms of carbon, nitrogen, and minerals. These nutrients don't nourish just the fungi. They also enter the soil, where they can be used by the organisms that live in the soil and the plants that draw nutrition from it.

THE PARTNERS

Symbiosis is a relationship between two unrelated life forms that live together and interact over a period of time. There are several kinds of symbiosis. When the interaction benefits both of the life forms, the symbiosis is known as mutualism. The two parties may be called symbionts or mutualists.

Many fungi live in mutualistic relationships with other living things. A lichen is a mutualistic symbiosis of a fungus and an alga or a blue-green bacterium. Another mutualism is the mycorrhiza, the union of a fungus with the roots of a plant. Mycorrhizae are not just common—they are almost universal. According to mycologist Tom Volk of the University of Wisconsin, more than 90 percent of the world's plants have mycorrhizae living in their roots.

There are two kinds of mycorrhizae. In an ectomycorrhiza (ecto means "outside"), the fungus forms a sheath, or snug wrapping, around the root. It sends fine tentacles into the root tissue, between the plant cells. It also stretches its hyphae outward, into the soil.

Ectomyrrhizae form on the roots of trees in a number of families, including pines, birches, oaks, spruces, and beeches. Many of the fungi in

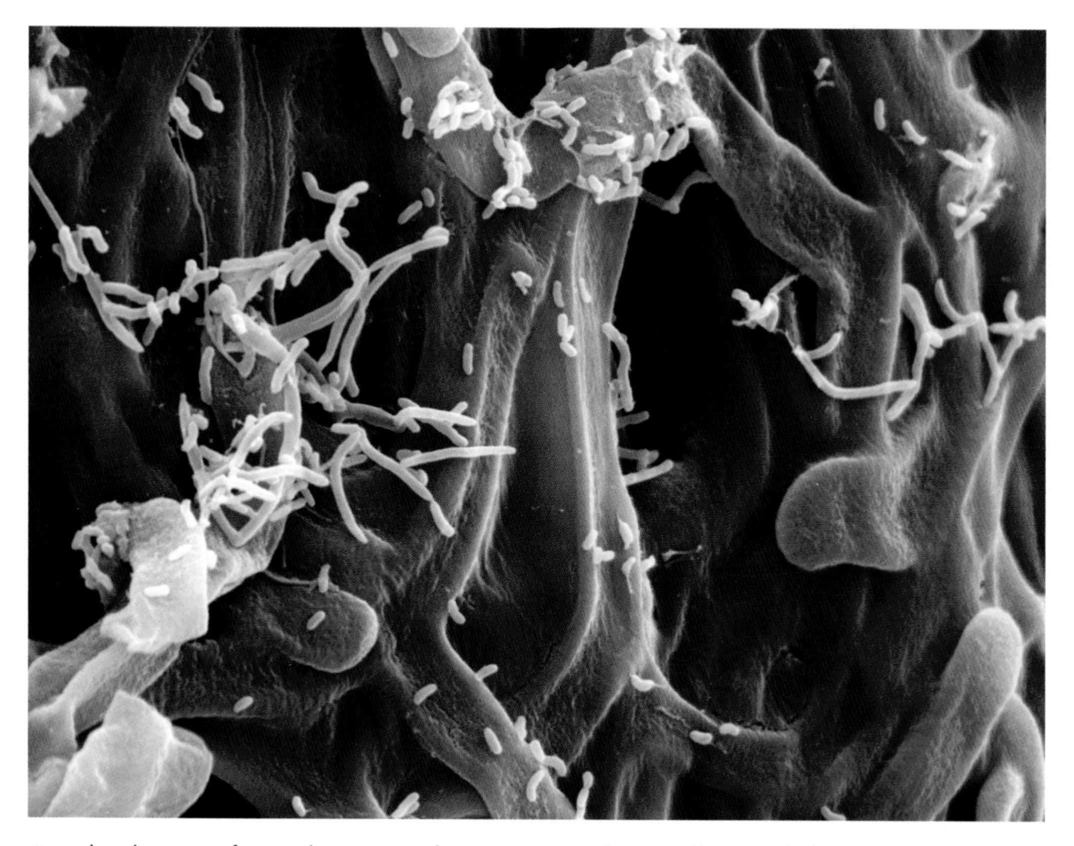

Found in the roots of most plants, mycorrhizae are unions between fungi and plants. A mycorrhiza forms when a mycelium penetrates a plant's root. In this image taken through an electron microscope, the light strands are the hyphae of a mycelium, and the darker bodies are roots.

ectomycorrhizae are species that produce large fruiting bodies. People have known for hundreds of years that certain mushrooms grow near certain kinds of plants. The beech-wood agaric mushroom, for example, is found close to beech trees. Scientists now know that this above-ground connection reflects what is happening below the surface, where the mycelia and the tree roots are joined to form mycorrhizae. About 40 percent of all the mushrooms in the world's forests are the fruiting bodies of ectomycorrhizae, according to mycologist Roy Watling of the Royal Botanical Garden in Edinburgh, Scotland.

In an endomycorrhiza (*endo* means "inside"), the fungus lives inside the root, and its hyphae enter the plant's cells. This is the more common kind of mycorrhiza. About 70 percent of plants in the world form endomycorrhizae. This includes all grasses, many other plants, and some trees.

In either kind of mycorrhiza, both the fungus and the plant benefit. The fungus may be protected from extremely cold or dry weather by the root. More important, the fungus gets a share of the food that the plant manufactures. In one study, mycorrhizae consumed 25 percent of the carbohydrates that a tree's leaves produced. Still, the tree benefited from the symbiosis. It was healthier than a similar tree without mycorrhizae.

Plants benefit from mycorrhizae in several ways. Fungal mycelia that are connected to a plant's roots act like extensions of its root system—they provide more surfaces through which the plant can absorb water and minerals from the soil. For this reason, plants with mycorrhizae do better than plants without mycorrhizae when growing conditions are difficult, such as during dry spells or in poor soil. In addition, many scientists think that the fungi in mycorrhizae give the plants some protection from other fungi that live in the soil, and perhaps also from plant-eating pests such as roundworms.

Mycorrhizae are always in roots, but fungi can form other symbiotic relationships with plants. Some fungi are called endophytes, which means "inside plants," because they live completely inside host plants, except when they send out spores. Fungi in the genus *Neotyphodium,* for example, live in grasses, but not in their roots. The fungus absorbs a small amount of the plant's food, and the plant is protected from hungry insects by chemicals that the fungus produces. Endophytes in grasses can be helpful or harmful to human interests, depending on how people want to use the grass. For landscaped areas such as golf courses, grass seed that is infected with the fungus cuts down on insect pest problems and the use of pesticides. But grass that will be used to feed livestock must be free of the fungus, because the fungus is toxic to animals.

Leaf-cutter ants tend their garden of white fungus. In addition to feeding the fungus freshly cut leaves, the ants groom it, removing any signs of mold as well as pests, such as other insects.

Fungi also form symbiotic relationships with animals. The leaf-cutter ants of South America are fungus farmers. The ants carry leaves into their nests, where the leaves become the food source for a special kind of fungus that lives only in the nests. Instead of spores, this fungus produces a liquid that the ants feed to their larvae. When a queen ant leads a migration to a new nest site, she carries a piece of the fungus mycelium inside her body. The fungus depends on the ants to provide it with food and with a way to spread from place to place. The ants depend on the fungus for food for their young. In Africa, termites cultivate fungus gardens in the same way. Certain species of beetles introduce fungi into the nests they hollow out in dead trees to hold their eggs. The fungus feeds on the dead wood and grows, so that when the eggs hatch, the beetle larvae have a supply of food close at hand. When the beetles mature and set off to lay their own eggs, they carry the fungus inside their bodies, introducing it to new substrates.

THE PARASITES

Parasitism is a relationship between two organisms that benefits one of them and harms the other. The organism that benefits is called the parasite, and the one that suffers is the host. Fungi are parasites on many kinds of hosts: algae, plants, insects, animals, and occasionally other fungi.

Fungi that parasitize plants are called plant pathogens, and the conditions they create are called plant diseases. Bacteria, viruses, and worms also infect plants with disease, but fungi may be the most serious plant pathogens. One study in Ohio, for example, found that about 150 plant diseases in the state were caused by bacteria and viruses, while fungi caused a thousand diseases.

Parasitic fungi attack many plants that have value to humans, such as food crops, trees, and ornamental plants. Grape powdery mildew, net blotch of barley, peach leaf curl, chestnut blight, apple blotch, and similar pathogens cause millions of dollars worth of damage each year. Cacao plants, the source of chocolate, suffer from plagues of several different fungal pathogens that can make the price of chocolate on the world market rise and fall.

The rusts and smuts that attack cereal grains are probably the most severe plant pathogens, because they strike at the staple food crops of much of the world's population. Plant breeders constantly try to develop new strains of cereal grains that have more resistance to such diseases as stem rust and stinking smut. The fungi keep evolving, too, adapting to meet the challenges of fungus-resistant crop strains and chemical pesticides.

Ergot fungus (the brown material) has infected this wheat. Ergot can occur in many types of cereal grains. Some historians think that outbreaks of poisoning caused by ergot-contaminated bread may have contributed to the witchcraft panics of earlier centuries.

One of the most widespread and destructive pathogens of grain is *Claviceps purpurea,* a sac fungus that can attack wheat, barley, oats, or rye anywhere in the world. Its common name is ergot. Town records from the European Middle Ages reveal outbreaks of terrible symptoms that were almost certainly caused by bread made from grain—especially rye—

Cordyceps is a genus of fungi that parasitize insects, such as this African ant. The fungus is growing out of the ant's antenna. It will eventually invade and consume the rest of the ant's body.

that was contaminated with ergot. Ergot poisoning can cause nausea, hallucinations, twitching, a feeling of ants crawling on the skin, and burning sensations in the limbs. It can also stop the blood flow to hands and feet, which sometimes turn black and fall off. One account from France in 994 says that "a plague of invisible fire broke out, cutting off limbs from the body and consuming many in a single night." Nearly a thousand years later, in 1951, a much smaller outbreak of ergot poisoning, also in France, was traced to bread made by a local baker. Modern farming and grain-processing methods, though, have made cases of ergot poisoning from food extremely rare.

Fungal parasites attack animals as well as plants. A few mushrooms are carnivorous, preying on small creatures such as insects and worms. *Pleurotus ostreatus* is an example. The fruiting body of this fungus is the edible oyster mushroom. Its mycelium paralyzes tiny worms with a toxin, then the hyphae work their way beneath the worms' skin to digest and consume the organs. Fungi in some other genera are equipped with small loops of sticky thread on their hyphae. These trap the worms, which the hyphae then invade and digest.

Most of the fungi that parasitize animals are microfungi, the species that remain tiny in all of their life stages. These parasitic fungi often enter the host's body as spores. They grow in the host's tissues and multiply. This can weaken the host, make it sick, or, in some cases, kill it.

At least three hundred species of fungi cause diseases in humans, according to Nicholas P. Money, a mycologist at Miami University in Ohio. They get into the body in various ways: from molds on food or household furnishings, carried by air or water, and through wounds such as scratches. Athlete's foot and ringworm are examples of fairly common mycoses. More deadly, and less common, is cryptococcosis, a disease of the lungs that can travel into the nervous system and the brain. People with weakened immune systems, such as AIDS patients and those who have had organ transplants, are especially vulnerable to this fungal infection and to some other mycoses as well. Fungal diseases are hard to treat because the drugs that affect fungi can also affect our animal cells. Bacteria are more different from animals than fungi are, which is one reason bacterial diseases are easier to treat than fungal ones.

Hundreds, if not thousands, of fungal spores are in and on our bodies all the time. Fortunately, most of them are harmless. Parasitism and mycosis are dangerous, but fungi have many other roles, both in the natural world and in human life and culture.

Dutch Elm Disaster

In 1918 and 1919, people in the European nation of Holland noticed that their elm trees were dying in large numbers. Leaves drooped, turned yellow, and died within days or weeks. Then whole branches died. A large, mature tree could die in less than two years.

World War I had just ended, after raging across Europe for four years. Some people thought that the trees were dying from the poison gas used against troops during the war—but trees were dying in areas that had never been exposed to gas. Soon two Dutch scientists discovered that the disease was caused by a fungus called *Ophiostoma ulmi.* The fungus had been carried to Europe from Dutch colonies in Southeast Asia in the late nineteenth century, probably as an unsuspected passenger in cargoes of tropical timber.

When *O. ulmi* infects a tree, it spreads along the network of tunnels that carry food and water throughout the tree. The hyphae of the fungus clog and block these passages, first the small ones, then the larger ones. Unable to get food and water, the tree dies. The fungal parasite lives on in its dead host, digesting the wood. But *O. ulmi* cannot travel easily from tree to tree unless the trees are close together and the root systems of the trees have grown together. The fungus alone did not cause the widespread destruction known as Dutch elm disease. It had help from elm bark beetles.

These beetles lay their eggs in the bark of dead elm trees. After the eggs hatch, the larvae burrow into the tree and feed on the wood until they turn into adult beetles and fly away looking for fresh leaves to eat. Beetles that grew up in elm trees killed by *O. ulmi* were covered with the fungus's spores when they came out of their burrows. They carried the spores to healthy trees and infected them.

Dutch elm disease was first spotted in North America in 1930. It probably crossed the ocean on shipments of elm logs. There were millions upon millions of elm trees in the United States and Canada, not only in forests but also in cities and towns. Elms were extremely popular as urban shade trees because they are tall and graceful, with spreading canopies of leaves. Soon these elms were under attack by the fungus and its transportation, the beetle. Planted in parks and along streets, the trees were often close enough together for their roots to join. In some places the fungus could spread even without the beetle.

Millions of American elms died in the twentieth century. The cost of removing and replacing them was enormous. Meanwhile, the fungus continued to travel. A shipment of infected elm logs sent from the United States to England in 1963, for example, launched an epidemic of Dutch elm disease that killed 25 million trees in the British Isles. Elm trees native to China and Siberia, however, turned out to be highly resistant to the disease. Today, tree breeders are developing hybrids by crossing these Asian elms with American and European elms. They are also trying to breed new, more disease-resistant varieties of American and European elms. Still, American elms will probably never again be as numerous, or as popular, as they were before the disaster of Dutch elm disease.

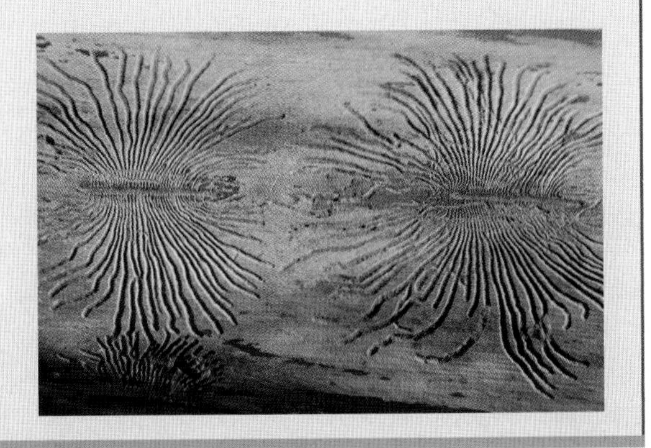

Galleries, or networks of tunnels, were gnawed beneath the bark of this elm tree by beetle larvae. Bark beetles helped spread a fungus that destroyed millions of elm trees—perhaps hundreds of millions—in North America and Europe during the twentieth century.

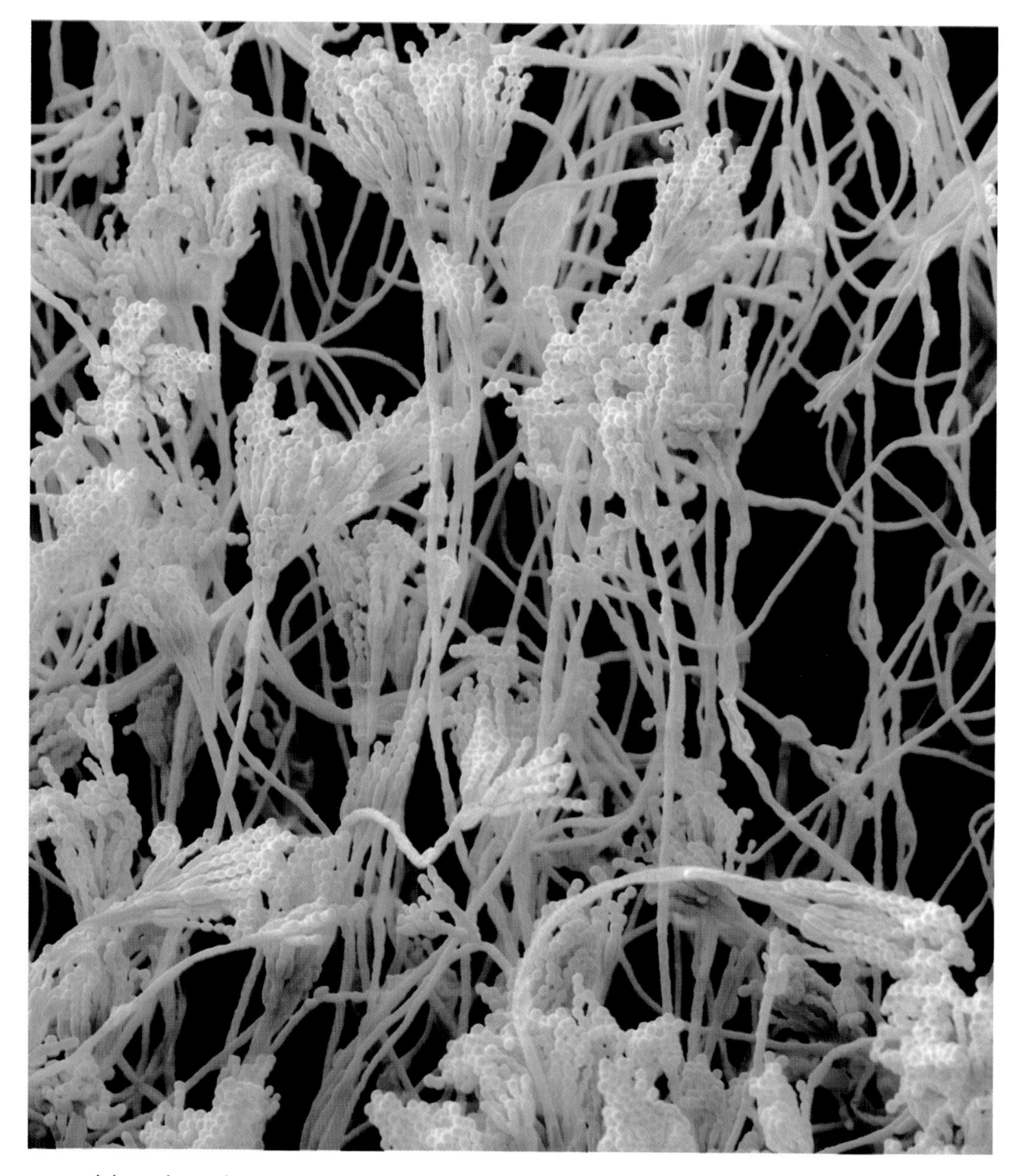

Viewed through an electron microscope, *Penicillium* mold resembles tangled yarn, with spore-producing bodies as tassels. This fungus evolved over millions of years to kill bacteria. In the mid-twentieth century, scientists harnessed that quality to save human lives. Who knows what other revolutionary discoveries the fungus kingdom may hold?

CHAPTER **FOUR**

Living with Fungi

"There was a fungus among us," American singer-songwriter Terry Noland said in 1958, in a pop song with that title. Noland was talking about a person, not a mushroom, but there *are* fungi among us—a lot of them. But because fungi are half a billion years old, and because there are probably more than a million and a half species of them, it might be more accurate to say that we are among them!

FUNGI IN FOOD

Agaricus bisporus, a medium-sized gilled mushroom that comes in brownish and white varieties, may be the world's most popular mushroom, or at least the one that is eaten most often. It has many common names, including button mushroom, table mushroom, white button, and—reflecting one of its uses—pizza mushroom. *A. bisporus* originated in France and is now commercially farmed in many parts of the world. Sold whole or in pieces, fresh, canned, or bottled, it is the only mushroom that some people ever eat.

A Thai mushroom farmer inspects his crop. Many—but not all—food mushrooms can be commercially grown.

Some popular edible mushrooms are brown and white buttons (lower right), oyster (lower left), portobellos (upper left), enokis (upper middle), and shiitakes (upper right).

But many other mushrooms are part of regional diets: porcinis in Italy, truffles in France, shiitakes and enokis in Japan, wood ear fungus in China, and termite mushrooms in Thailand, for example. As global travel and trade introduce these and other edible fungi to new consumers, stores around the world are beginning to offer more varieties.

Worldwide, mushroom farming is a big business. Most commercially cultivated mushrooms are grown in beds of compost, such as sawdust or straw mixed with chicken manure. In China, shiitakes are cultivated in

A truffle hunter's trusty sidekick is a pig trained to sniff out the world's most expensive mushrooms, which grow underground in the roots of oak trees.

fields of hardwood logs that have been packed with spore-containing material and left to lie in the open. Mycelia grow inside the logs, and mushrooms appear on the surface. The French encourage the growth of truffles, the world's most expensive mushrooms, by planting and cultivating oak seedlings, because truffles are the fruiting bodies of mycorrhizae that form on the roots of oak trees. The truffles themselves cannot be seen—they are underground. Truffle hunters usually locate them with the help of dogs or pigs trained to sniff out the fungi.

Chanterelles, matsutake, and other desirable mushrooms have not yet been successfully farmed. They must be gathered in the wild. Picking wild mushrooms has become another commercial industry. Collectors gather the fungi, often in national forests or on public land, then sell them to

The common morel, sometimes called a sponge mushroom, is not only edible but, in the opinion of many mushroom lovers, delicious. Gathered in woodlands, morels are especially numerous after forest fires.

buyers, who in turn sell them to mushroom brokers for national or even international distribution. Mushroom hunting is not always a matter of business, however. Many people occasionally gather a few mushrooms for their own use. The gathering and eating of wild mushrooms can be dangerous, though, because many toxic species resemble safe ones. No one should pick or taste a wild mushroom without expert guidance.

People eat the fruiting bodies of larger fungi, but they use microfungi to make a variety of other foods. Yeast is essential to the making of bread and beer, and all other alcoholic drinks—it makes the ingredients ferment, a necessary chemical change. The industrial manufacture of certain food flavorings, such as the citric acid that is used in many soft drinks and other products, also depends on fungal fermentation.

FUNGI AS MEDICINE AND DRUGS

People have used some of the larger fungi as medicine for a long time. The ancient Romans, for example, knew that applying certain puffballs to wounds could help with healing. These fungi produce chemicals that kill bacteria and may prevent infection.

Traditional Chinese medicine is especially rich in mushroom-based remedies. Medical researchers are now studying some of these remedies to identify any healing properties they possess. They have already learned that shiitake mushrooms, an ingredient in many Chinese and Japanese herbal medicines, contain a compound called lentinan that has good effects in treating some kinds of cancer tumors. *Ganoderma lucidum,* another mushroom used by Asian herbalists for hundreds of years, may turn out to have similar benefits.

Microfungi have played a vital role in modern medicine ever since 1928, when British medical researcher Alexander Fleming discovered that a fungus called *Penicillium* could kill the bacteria that cause staph infections. The fungus proved to produce an antibacterial compound called

Alexander Fleming in his London laboratory. Fleming discovered in 1928 that *Penicillium* mold kills dangerous bacteria. Some stories say the discovery occurred when a window was accidentally left open, letting mold spores drift onto a dish of bacteria.

penicillin. This new "wonder drug" reached large-scale production in the early 1940s, just in time to save many people wounded in World War II from dying of infection. More recently, cyclosporin (used in organ transplants and to treat some diabetics) and statin drugs (which help prevent heart disease by controlling cholesterol in the blood) have been developed from microfungi.

Since ancient times, some fungi have been recognized for their intoxicating properties. In traditional religious practices in places as far apart as Siberia and the Amazon, people have altered their mental states by eating mushrooms, or by drinking liquids made from them. Depending upon the mushroom and the dose, the effects can include nausea, dizziness, euphoria (a feeling of happiness), and hallucinations. Some people use mushrooms as intoxicants today, although their effects are unpredictable and can be dangerous.

OTHER USES

Fungi have had a variety of traditional uses in various parts of the world. Mushroom-based dyes, usually in shades of red, yellow, or brown, are used to color wool. The fibers of some shelf fungi can be made into paper, and the fibers of tinder fungus can be woven into cloth.

Today, researchers are looking at ways of using fungi to control pests. Fungi are known to cause disease in plants, animals, and even other fungi—why not turn that destructive power to productive use? A good example is the microfungus *Beauveria bassiana,* which causes an ailment called muscadine disease in silkworms. More than two thousand years ago, Chinese silk producers complained that this disease was killing their prized silkworms. Since the late twentieth century, however, the Chinese have used the fungus, under careful control, to kill insect pests such as corn borers and leafhoppers. Another biocontrol agent—a natural weapon against pests—is a strain of fungus from Israel that is being used against the destructive lucerne aphid in Australia.

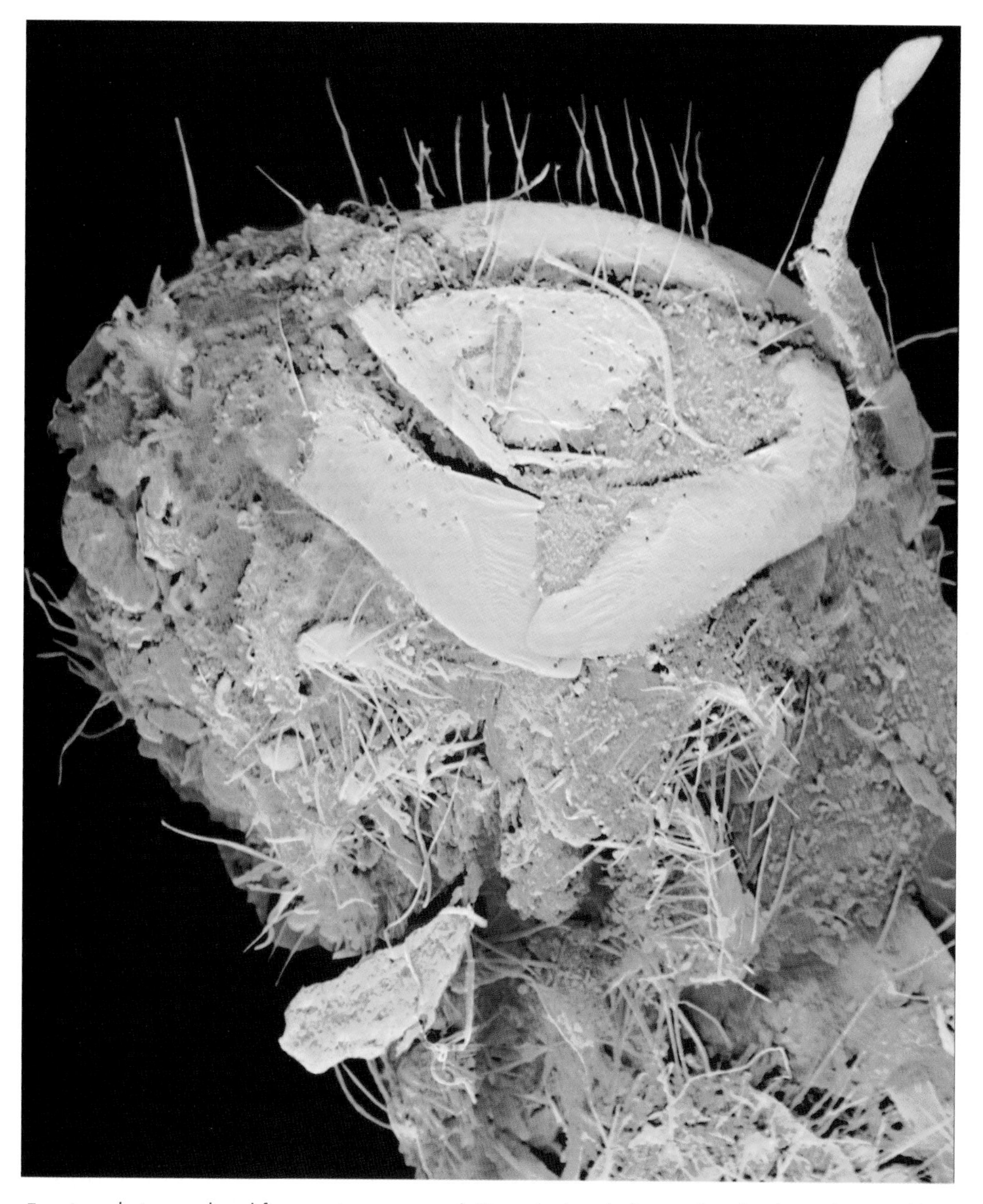

Fungi are being explored for uses in pest control. Here, the head of a maybug has been destroyed by a fungus (shown in green). The fungus targets the insect but not the crops on which the insects feed.

Bioprospecting is the search for useful or profitable compounds in living things. Fungi are of great interest to bioprospectors because they have been less thoroughly studied than plants. Fungi may hold a world of unknown but beneficial properties, not just in pest control but in food production and medicine as well.

CONSERVATION

In 2006 the World Conservation Union, an international organization that tracks the status of species around the world, had only three fungi on its Red List of endangered and threatened species. Two were lichens, and one was a mushroom. This was fewer than for any other group of organisms on the list. Good news for the fungi, right?

Not necessarily. Only three species of fungi had been fully evaluated by the organization. That means that 100 percent of the fungi that were evaluated were found to be threatened.

Fungi as a group are not considered critically endangered, or even threatened. Mycologists point out, however, that taking a census of the fungi is complicated. For one thing, many fungi are invisible—they are either microscopically small, or they are mycelia that live inside their substrates. People can identify and count the fruiting bodies of the larger fungi, but this gives an incomplete picture of how individual species are doing. In addition, only a small percentage of fungi are known. Whole groups could be disappearing before they are even identified.

Most experts agree that collecting fruiting bodies, even large-scale picking of wild mushrooms, is not a serious danger to fungi, although some governments have taken steps to limit or control it. The real threats are habitat loss and pollution, which affect fungi along with every other organism in an ecosystem. For example, some ingredients in fertilizers, especially nitrogen, have been shown to harm mycorrhizae. And the loss

A toadstool serves as a frog's umbrella. Like this frog, nearly all creatures alive today share their ecosystems with fungi. The fungus kingdom is a frontier with much exploration yet to be done before scientists fully understand the many complex roles that fungi play in the world of living things.

of woodlands and grasslands, as well as other ecological niches such as moss beds, can mean the loss of fungi along with plants.

Scientists are learning that fungi are woven into the fabric of life in subtle, important, and sometimes unexpected ways. They are recyclers, food sources, pathogens, and partners in plant growth. From tropical rain forests to deserts, members of the fungus kingdom are part of every ecosystem that the conservationists of the world want to protect.

The Ice Man's Fungi

In 1991, a pair of vacationers from Germany were hiking in the Alps, on the border between Austria and Italy, when they discovered a mummified body. It turned out to be the remains of a man who died in the mountains more than five thousand years ago. The ice preserved him after his death, until it melted enough to reveal him to the hikers.

Ötzi the Iceman, as he came to be called, is one of the most complete mummies ever found. His garments and possessions were found with him. Scholars and scientists were thrilled to have a rare glimpse of the clothes and equipment used by prehistoric Europeans. Mycologists took a special interest, because among the items Ötzi carried in his "toolkit" are three pieces of fungus.

One is a chunk of tinder fungus, a type of shelf fungus that catches fire but smolders, or burns slowly without flames. People in many parts of the world have used tinder fungus as a lightweight, portable fuel for starting fires. It can also be used for carrying fire from place to place.

Ötzi's other two mycological items are also pieces of shelf fungus, but they are from a different species, *Piptoporus betulinus.* One piece is a cone about 2 inches (5 centimeters) long. The other is a ball of about the same size. Holes have been drilled through them, and each is strung on a leather thong. These pieces of fungus must have been important to Ötzi, but what was their purpose?

The leading theory is that they were his medicine chest. *Piptoporus* has antiseptic qualities. It produces substances that clean wounds and help them heal. Some reports say that it also reduces pain and fatigue. Researchers think that Ötzi might have rubbed the cone-shaped piece on scratches and cuts, and sucked on the larger one. Ötzi's medicine chest was not enough to save his life, though. His body shows signs of knife wounds, and a flint arrowhead was found embedded in his back.

Fungus has played another role in the story of the Iceman. His body and many of his possessions are dead organic matter, exactly what many fungi live on. As soon as he was exposed to air, spores germinated on him, and fungus began to develop. In the hope of preventing further decay, Ötzi is now kept in a climate-controlled chamber. It is more high-tech than the glacier that covered him for so many centuries, but just as cold.

A five-thousand-year-old mummy found in the Alps in 1991 carried two pieces of this type of fungus, *Piptosporus betulinus,* or the birch polypore. The fungus has antiseptic properties and may have served this prehistoric European as a portable first-aid kit.

GLOSSARY

adapt—To change or develop in ways that aid survival in the environment.

alga—A one-celled or multicelled plantlike organism generally found in water; usually classified in kingdom of protists.

ancestral—Having to do with lines of descent or earlier related forms.

conservation—Action or movement aimed at protecting and preserving wildlife or its habitat.

decompose—To break down dead plant and animal material into organic compounds in the environment that can be reused.

eukaryote—Organism made of cells that have a distinct nucleus.

evolution—Genetic change in life over time as new species, or types of plants and animals, develop from old ones.

evolve—To change genetically over time.

extinct—No longer existing; died out.

flagellum—Whiplike extension of a cell that moves as a result of chemical processes in the cell.

fruiting body—A form the fungus takes for sexual reproduction, also called a sporangium, or sporocarp.

genetic—Having to do with genes, material made of DNA inside the cells of living organisms. Genes carry information about inherited characteristics from parents to offspring and determine the form of each organism.

hypha—A filament that grows out from a spore; a mass of hyphae is a mycelium.

lichen—An organism that consists of a fungus and an alga; together they form the thallus, or lichen body.

microscopic—Extremely small; seen clearly (or at all) only through a microscope.

mushroom—The fruiting body of certain kinds of fungi.

mycelium—A mass of hyphae.

mycology—The scientific study of fungi.

mycorrhiza—The symbiotic union of a fungus and the roots of a plant.

organism—Any living thing.

paleontology—The study of ancient life, mainly through fossils.

parasite—An orgnaism that eats material from a living plant or animal host and harms the host.

pesticide—A substance that kills pests.

prokaryote—An organism made up of cells that do not have a distinct nucleus; bacteria are prokaryotes.

saprotroph—A fungus that lives by digesting dead plant or animal material.

spore—A tiny structure that spreads genetic material and that can grow into another fungus.

substrate—A substance on and in which a fungus grows and feeds.

symbiosis—The relationship between two organisms that live closely together; a mutualistic symbiosis benefits both organisms.

taxonomy—The scientific system for classifying living things, grouping them in categories according to similarities and differences, and naming them.

vegetative body—The main, non-reproductive body of the fungus; also called thallus.

FUNGUS KINGDOM

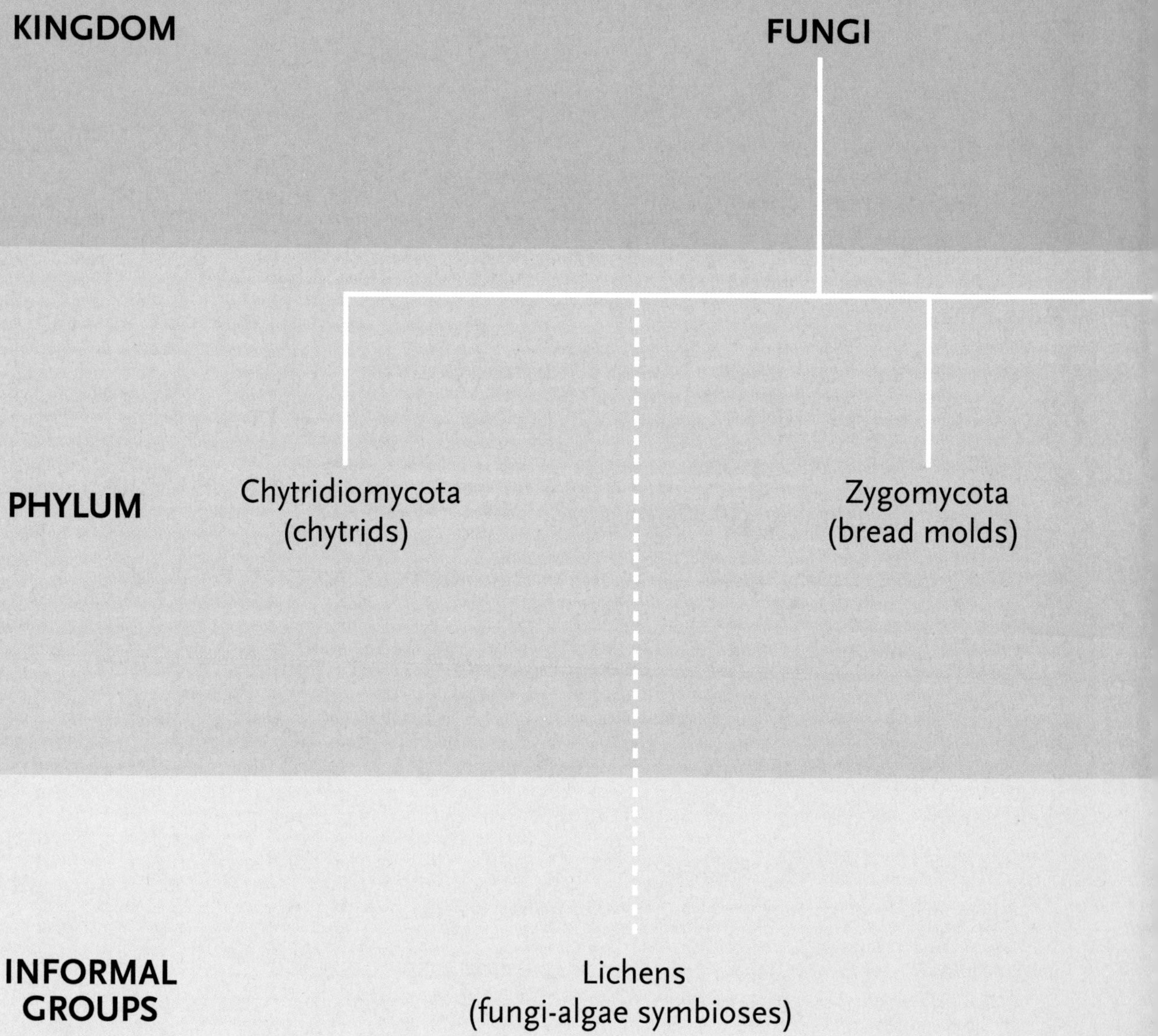

KINGDOM	FUNGI
PHYLUM	Chytridiomycota (chytrids); Zygomycota (bread molds)
INFORMAL GROUPS	Lichens (fungi-algae symbioses)

FAMILY TREE

Ascomycota (yeasts and sac fungi)

Basidiomycota (club fungi)

Deuteromycota (fungi that cannot reproduce sexually)

FURTHER READING

Ball, Jackie. *Protists and Fungi.* Milwaukee, WI: Gareth Stevens, 2004.

Brock, David L. *Infectious Fungi.* Philadelphia, PA: Chelsea House Publishers, 2006.

Pascoe, Elaine. *Slime, Molds, and Fungi*. Woodbridge, CT: Blackbirch, 1999.

Phillips, Roger. *Mushrooms and Other Fungi of North America.* Buffalo, NY: Firefly, 2005.

Watling, Roy. *Fungi.* Washington, D.C.: Smithsonian Books, 2003.

WEB SITES

http://herbarium.usu.edu/fungi/FunFacts/factindx.htm
Hosted by the Utah State University Intermountain Herbarium, this kid-friendly site is called Fun Facts About Fungi. It has fungi-related information, experiments, and games.

http://www.perspective.com/nature/fungi/
The Fungus Kingdom has brief overviews of many of the major groups of fungi, with many color photos.

http://tomvolkfungi.net/
Tom Volk of the Biology Department at the University of Wisconsin, La Cross, has maintained the Tom Volk's Fungi page for years. Packed with information and photos, it features a Fungus of the Month.

http://tolweb.org/Fungi/2377
The Fungi page of the Internet Tree of Life Project has sections on features, fossils, famous fungi, and taxonomy.

http://www.ucmp.berkeley.edu/fungi/fungi.html
Introduction to the Fungi, maintained by the University of California Museum of Paleontology, has brief entries on fungal evolution, classification, structure, and ecology.

http://www.mycolog.com/fifthtoc.html
The Fifth Kingdom web site offers an online version of a mycology textbook, with photographs. Its Frequently Asked Questions section is a good starting point.

http://www.sciencenewsforkids.org/articles/20050713/Feature1.asp
Fungus Hunt, an article on the Science News for Kids web site, combines basic fungus facts with news about current research in mycology, including medical studies of mushrooms.

http://ocid.nacse.org/lichenland
Lichenland, a web site developed by Oregon State University, offers a kid-friendly introduction to lichens, organisms made up of fungi and algae.

BIBLIOGRAPHY

The author found these books especially helpful when researching this book.

Carlile, Michael J., Sarah C. Watkinson, and Graham W. Gooday. *The Fungi.* 2nd edition. San Diego, CA: Academic Press, 2001.

Deacon, J.W. *Modern Mycology*. 3rd edition. Oxford, UK: Blackwell Science, 1997.

Hudler, George W. *Magical Mushrooms, Mischievous Molds.* Princeton, NJ: Princeton University Press, 1998.

Kirk, P.M., et al, editors. *Ainsworth and Bisby's Dictionary of the Fungi.* 9th edition. New York: CABI, 2001.

Money, Nicholas P. *Mr. Bloomfield's Orchard: The Mysterious World of Mushrooms, Molds, and Mycologists.* New York: Oxford University Press, 2002.

Moore, David. *Slayers, Saviors, Servants, and Sex: An Exposé of Kingdom Fungi.* New York: Springer-Verlag, 2001.

INDEX

Page numbers in **boldface** are illustrations and charts.

aflatoxin, 28
agaric, 21, **21, 36,** 43, 61
Agaricus bisporus, 71
algae, 30, 33, 34
Amanita, 12-13, **13,** 21, **21, 36,** 55
amber, 21, 22, **22**
ants, 63, **63**
Armarilla ostoyae, **6,** 7-8, 41
asci, 28, 49
Ascomycota, 28-29, **29,** 32, 49
ascospores, 49
athlete's foot, 39, **39**

bacteria, 23, 30, 38, 60, 64
Basidiomycota, 29, **30,** 32, 43, 49
basidiospores, 49-50
Beauveria bassiana, 78
bioluminescence, 37-38, **38**
bioprospecting, 80
blights, 8, 64
bracket fungi, 29

chitin, 38
Chromista, 33
Chytridiomycota, 25-26, **26,** 48, 49, 51
cladogram, 14-15
classification, 8-15
Claviceps purpurea, 65-66, **65**
club fungus, 29, 30
conservation, 80-81
crops, 64, 65, **65,** 66, 78
cyclosporin, 78

death cap, 12, 13, **13**
decomposers, 8, 25, 28, 33, 59-60, **59**
Deuteromycota, 32
Devonian period, 20, 21, 34
disease, 8, 25, 28, 32, **32,** 33, 67
dry rot, 57, 58, **58**
Dutch elm disease, 68-69, **69**

ectomycorrhizae, 60
edible fungus, 28, 71-76
    See also food
endangerment, 80
endomycorrhizae, 62
endophytes, 62
ergot, 65-66, **65**
eukaryotes, 24, 32-33

fermentation, 76
flagellae, 25, **26,** 51
Fleming, Alexander, 76-78, **77**
food, 8, 27, **27,** 28, 29, 65-66, **65,** 67,
    71-76, **72, 73, 74, 75**
fossil, 20-23, **20, 21, 22,** 34-35, **35,**
    82-83
fruiting body, 40-45, **41, 42, 43, 44,** 61
fungal infections, 25, 32, **32, 39,** 67
fungus gardens, 63-64

Ganoderma lucidum, 76
genetics, 14, 15, 46, 47, 48
geographic distribution, 46
gills, 43-44 **43**
Glomeromycota, 28, 49
grains, 28, 51, 64, 65, **65,** 66

history, 9-11, 14, 19-24, 37-38, 55
humans and fungus, 25, 32, **32, 39,** 57, 65-66, 67, 68, 69
hyphae, 39-40, **39, 40,** 48, 49, 51, 57, 58, **58,** 60, 67, 69

imperfect fungi, 32, **32,** 49
insects, 27, 33, **33,** 51, 52, 53, **53,** 55, 63-64, **63, 66,** 68, 69, **68,** 78, 79, **79**
intoxicants, 78

jelly fungus, 29, 30, **30**

lichen, 30-31, **30, 31,** 34
Linnaeus, Carolus, 10-11, 23

medicine, 8, 18, 28, 76-78, **77**
microfungi, 59, 67, 76
microsporidia, 28
mildew, 8, 33, 64
mold, 8, 27, **27,** 31
monerans, 23, 24
morels, 28, 44, 75, **75**
mushroom, **6,** 7-8, 21, **22,** 29, 37, 71-76, **72, 73, 74, 75**
carnivorous, 67
farms, 72, **72,** 73
gathering, 74, **74,**, 75, **75**
giant, 34-35, **35**
structure, 42-46 **42, 43**
mutualism, 60
mycelium, 39-43, 47, 48, 62, 63, 67
formation, 40, **40**
Mycena lucentipes, 38, **38**
mycorrhizae, 60-62, **61**

nucleus, 23, 38

Ophiostoma ulmi, 68-69

Palaeomyces, 20-21, **20**
parasite, 8, 20, 57, 58, 62, 64-69, **65, 66, 69**
Penicillium See penicillin
penicillin, **18, 28,** 70, 76-78, **77**
pesticides, 62, 64, 78, **79**
phyla (of fungus), 25
phylogenetics, 14-15
plants, 20, 21, 23, 27, 28, 35, 38
poisonous (fungus), 12, 13, **13,** 36, **36,** 55, 62, 65-66, **65**
polypore, 82-83, **83**
porcinis, 73
Potter, Beatrix, 31
prokaryotes, 24, 38
Prototaxites, 34-35, **35**
protists, 23, 24, 28
puffball, **10,** 11, 29, 44, 53, 54, **54**

reproduction, 46-54, **48, 50, 52, 53, 54**
asexual, 46-49, **48**
sexual, 25, 32, 40, 46, 49-54, **50, 52, 53, 54**
Rhizopus, 27, 28

Rhynie chert, 20-21, **20**
ringworm, 32, **32**
roots, 27, 28, 60, 62
rusts, 64

sac fungi, 28-29, **29,** 30, 44, 48, 49
scavengers, 59-60, **59**
scientific names, 10, 11, 12, 14
Serpula lacrymans, 57-58
shelf fungus, 37, 45, **45,** 56, **56**
shiitakes, 73, **73**
size, 7, 44, 45
slime molds, 32, 33
smuts, 64
soil, 25, 27
species, 30, 47
  number of, 19-20
sporangia, 48, 49
spore, 28, 43, 45, 48, 49, 50-54, **50, 52, 54,** 63, 67, 68, 74
  prints, 54
sporocarp *See* fruiting body
Stramenopila, 33
structure (of fungus), 38-46, **39, 40, 41, 42, 43,** 44, 45
symbiosis, 30, 60-64, **61, 63**

taxonomic chart, **16-17, 86-87**
taxonomy, 8-15
thallus *See* mycelium
toadstool, 8, 29, 55
trees, 34, 60, 62, 64, 68-69, **69**
truffles, 28, 29, 43, 73, 74, **74**
Tuber magnatum, 29
tubes, 45

underground, 7, 8

Vendian period, 21, 25

water, 25, 29, 51
  molds, 32, 33, **33**
Web sites, 89
wood, 34, 57, 58, **58,** 60, 64

yeast, 8, 28, 29, 47-48, **48,** 76

Zygomycota, 27-28, **27,** 48, 49

ABOUT THE AUTHOR

Rebecca Stefoff is the author of a number of books on scientific subjects for young readers. She has explored the world of plants and animals in Marshall Cavendish's Living Things series and in several volumes of the AnimalWays series, also published by Marshall Cavendish. For the Family Trees series, she has authored books on primates and flowering plants. Stefoff has also written about evolution in *Charles Darwin and the Evolution Revolution* (Oxford University Press, 1996), and she appeared in the *A&E Biography* program on Darwin and his work. Stefoff lives in Portland, Oregon. You can learn more about her and her books for young readers at www.rebeccastefoff.com.